On the Establishment of the Republic

Published by Sacra Press.

Francesco Patrizi, *On the Establishment of the Republic.*
Translated by Richard Robinson.
Typed, edited, & designed by Cody Justice.
© 2025 by Sacra Press

Sacra Press
www.sacrapress.com
contact@sacrapress.com or sacrapress@gmail.com

First edition.
Printed in the United States of America.

Go to www.sacrapress.com
for more reformed, right-wing, & classic books, music, and art,
to become a subscriber, to commission a work, and more.

Godspeed and goodwar.

On the Establishment of the Republic

by
Francesco Patrizi

Translated by
Richard Robinson

Edited by
Cody Justice

SACRA PRESS

Contents

Epistle Dedicatory

TO THE Right Worshipful and His Singular Good Master, Sir William Allen Knight, Alderman of the City of London: Richard Robinson, His Humble Servant & Faithful Orator, Wisheth Long Life, Prosperous Health, Increase of Worship, and Perpetual Felicity.

Solomon, that peerless prince of prudence (right Worshipful), among his pithy parables persuading to the searching forth of wisdom and her fruits, saith: The path of the Righteous shineth as the light, that is ever brighter and brighter, unto the perfect day: but the way of the ungodly is as the darkness; they know not where they fall. Doubtless as every age hath either had his integrity or imperfection, wherein as well the felicity as indemnity of human estate hath appeared, more or less, to be praised for the worthiness, or pitied for the wretchedness: so is it a true testimony of the inestimable love of God lent toward those which, being duly directed in the path of perfection, do nothing digress therefrom, but persist constant unto the end, rather increasing than impairing their felicity: and, on the other part, where such as either reject their calling, or withstand the wisdom of God, do walk in byways and wander in willful darkness. Who hath not seen that the indignation of God hath been evidently poured upon them, scattering them, and overthrowing them even in their own wickedness?

The proof whereof approacheth even until these present days, in such sort among Christians, that if Heraclitus, the heathen philosopher, were now again living, and should but once step out at his doors to view the state and condition of the time present (whereas in his days he wept but by fits, to see the infelicity of that age), I verily suppose he would now continually shed tears abundantly without stinting, to see the ruinous decay of Christianity in this later age: and I doubt also, if Democritius were again living, and did behold the doings of both sorts of people in the world, whether he would laugh for joy in contemplating of the prosperous estate of the best Christians, or deride the froward fortune of the most wicked and ungodly at this day. Albeit throughout Christendom now, what kingdom, country, or common weale appeareth altogether so peaceable and prosperous, which hath not been lately, or is not presently encumbered with obscurity and absurdity of life and manners? as some walking in the righteous path have their light emblemished by others of the house of iniquity: some fain would walk the true path, and with civil dissension are separated from their godly purposes. But the greater part, no doubt, refusing light for darkness, do so nuzzle themselves in wickedness, that they labor with malignity to work a confused chaos of Christianity in general. In the midst of whom, behold (right Worshipful) greatly to the admiration of the rest, about us, but more to our private consolation, and most of all to the glory of the immortal God, the unspeakable love and eternal good grace of his blessing, appeareth in most bright beams of his blissful bounty, overshadowing this our native country of England, with far more superabundant felicities than many other nations: namely, by so long, peaceable, and prosperous courses of Christ's Gospel—that infallibly lamp of light, directed and protected by so peerless and precious a princess, so godly and gracious a governess, our most Christian and dearest sovereign, Lady Queen Elizabeth, assisted with so many crystal stars of stately light under her, garnishing and safeguarding the good government of this her majesty's realm and dominions of the same, with most wholesome, godly, and politic laws and constitutions, for the continual conservation of the public weale thereof universally, free from all private prejudice and public perturbation. This then so surpassing felicity duly considered, what subject is not throughly enforced, freely to utter and express the received comfort which he feeleth inwardly and seeth so apparently?

Verily when I, the meanest member of thousands, revolve this benefit in my mind, and see how far beyond the expectation and deserts of man, the providence of God dealeth with us, thus still preserving us and suffering others to quayle in their froward fortunes and calamities: being inwardly lightened with a certain secret consolation in one respect, and outwardly with painful pen pitying and deploring the state of the other: as duty chiefly bindeth me, I have at this present enforced my study (though as a Pigmeian in simple power) to practice somewhat with Hercules, or as otherwise desirous to travel with Ulysses, to win (albeit with weariness) somewhat if it were possible, by any good means, to benefit this bulwark of beatitude (this my native country, I mean) which, with such multitude of worthy practitioners notwithstanding, is already made famous, yet ceased I not with Sysiphus to roule the stone, but in such penury of power, as Architas the Philosopher attributing to be the appropriate discommodity to dexterity of wit, which I deny to be remaining in me, I have hazarded my poor hap in such simple handiwork (as I could, though not so well as I would) in translating out of Latin into English, nine books of the godly, reverend, and learned FRANCIS PATRICIUS, Bishop of Gaeta in Italy: whose works in the worthiness thereof reviving the author, dead threescore years ago and upwards, were in the Latin tongue by him left and entitled by the name of commentaries of the institution, state, and government of a common weale. Which albeit it contain profane principles of old time, interlaced with the actions, opinions, examples, counsels, sentences, and sayings of heathen emperors, kings, princes, captains, orators, philosophers, and such like, for the direction of mundane matters in civil government, with the learned opinion of the author discoursing upon every particularity: yet therein is copy of matter worth memory and imitation for every estate and member of a good Christian common weale at this day. And because it briefly so toucheth good order, in maintenance of a monarchy and the government thereof: I have entitled it, *A Moral Method of Civil Policy*, prefixing the particular contents before every book, with annotations in the margin, reducing the same into one table alphabetical, for the more direct assertion of the particularities in every several book.

But this by my rash attempt at the first so boldly begun, in continuance so bluntly done and finished, neither beautified nor burnished with any buxsomness of apt and eloquent English phrase: fearing much mine own imeprfection therein, I labored not only to have the same surveyed but also supplied with more learned skill and authority, before I would hazard the publishing thereof. Which when I had obtained, even then bethinking me on whom I might best bestow the benefit of this my simple travail: beyond the deserts of all others, considering with myself the manifest benefits which I have received from time to time these twelve years at your Worship's bountiful hands: I deemed myself a debtor even in duty to dedicate the same unto you, as a testimony of my thankful, serviceable, and well wishing heart towards you, as a pledge of the faithful zeal that I bear to this famous city of London, whereof you are an ancient Magistrate, and I your poor servant a simple member of the same: and consequently, as an earnest token of my unfeigned goodwill and true meaning towards this my native country.

Beseeching your Worship, and all other well meaning Magistrates, to pardon my bold rudeness herein, and to accept well in worth my poor goodwill, and well meaning mind, as wishing unto you especially that this my simple mite were in value more worth than Midas his golden diadem, to be thrown into the treasury of your worthy deserts: and as if this my poor present, were more in price, than a purchased prize of precious smaradges from India (had they so luckily light in my lot) I could willingly at this present vouchsafe to the enriching of this my native country: yet nevertheless (such as it is) pretending simply and sincerely, wishing herein to profit and pleasure all men, and not to disprofit nor displease any, I yield the same to be shielded under God's good pleasure and your worthy patronage. Concluding with dutiful and hearty prayer unto the Almighty, for the long and prosperous preservation of our most gracious sovereign Lady the Queen's majesty, and her honorable counselors: for the flourishing estate of this our public weale in every degree, where, including the welfare and felicity of this honorably city: by dutiful remembrance I pray especially amongst all others, that your Worship, my good Lady and Mistress, your loving wife, and all your children, may enjoy long and happy days on earth, and in fine, the most assured habitacle of perdurable felicities. Amen.

Your Worship's most humble servant and faithful orator,

RICHARD ROBINSON

Quantus Patritio debet Respublica grates,
Cui suus hoc studio vindice constat honos,
Aureus hic monstrat (vel me reticente) libellus,
Ingenio, genio, divite et arte scatens.

Hinc morum species, hinc dogmata pura petuntur,
Hinc vitae elicitur ciuica norma piae.
Historiae quicquid Latiae, memorántue Pelasgae
Vtile, Patritius sedulus exposuit.

Dia celebratur dignis Concordia phthongis,
Dissidij hic{que} lues pingitur atra trucis.
Hic bene perspicimus vestigia trita Sophorum,
Quam{que} malèa priscis degeneramus auis.

Qui praesunt summae rerum, et moderantur habenas,
Ex isto exugent cōmoda magna libro.
Primates Regni, Symmistae, bella gerentes,
Artifices{que} etiam hic quo doceantur, habent.

Deni{que} Rex et Grex, populus, promiscua plebs{que}
Permagnum hinc possunt conciliare decus.
Ifoelix Liber, i, dextra contexte Minerua,
Digne teri à cunctis clima per omne viris.

—Thomas Newton, Cestreshyrius

How greatly does the Republic owe thanks to Patritius,
By whose zealous defense its honor is preserved!
This golden little book (even if I were silent)
Proclaims itself, teeming with wit, genius, and rich artistry.

Here, the forms of conduct, here, pure doctrines are sought;
From it, the rule of a holy civic life is drawn.
Whatever is useful in Latin or Pelasgian histories
Patritius has diligently set forth.

Sacred harmony is celebrated with fitting tones,
And the dark plague of cruel discord is depicted here.
Here we clearly see the well-worn paths of the wise,
And how shamefully we degenerate from our ancient ancestors.

Those who preside over the highest affairs and guide the reins
May draw great advantages from this book.
The kingdom's leaders, counselors, warriors in battle,
Even artisans, may here find what instructs them.

Finally, king and flock, people and common multitude,
Can from this source procure great honor.
Unlucky book, go, woven by the hand of Minerva,
Worthy to be handled by men in every clime.

—Thomas Newton, Cestreshyrius

Certain Notes

SELECTED OUT OF THE PREFACE OF FRANCISCUS PATRITIUS SENENSIS, BISHOP OF GAETA, INTO HIS BOOK OF THE INSTITUTION, STATE, AND GOVERNMENT OF A COMMON WEALE

THE PLEASANTNESS of the soil wherein the city Gaeta standeth, the marvelous fruitfulness of that country, and the wonderful wholesomeness of the air, fostereth and nourisheth men long and many years in health: therefore the words of Scipio Africanus are the less to be marveled at, in saying, that he became young and waxed, as it were, a child again, when he together with his friend, Laelius, gathered and picked up little round smooth stones at Gaeta.

Nothing better showeth what a man is than his speech: for it openeth the sense or meaning of his mind, and expresseth the devices of the same, which both is divine and is also confessed and known to be the best and chiefest part of man. Hereunto tendeth the wise saying of Socrates, when as he said these words unto a young man that held his peace: speak, said he, that I may see what thou art. Meaning hereby that a man is not to be considered and deemed by the outward lineaments and feature of his body and face, but by the inward disposition and quality of his mind.

As it is gladsome and acceptable for wayfaring men to tread in their steps which have walked well afore them: so it is unto a good governor to direct his course that way, whereby many afore have easily arrived to the having of their desires.

We see all the best writers in every excellent art have been, as it were, spited, ill reported, and torn in pieces by backstabbers: and namely Homer, who, notwithstanding he was the father of all poets and the grand captain of all disciplines, yet had he many enemies and spiteful carpers, especially on Zoylus of Macedonia, who, presuming to prefer his own rusty wit before the golden vein of that divine poet, saucily inveighed by writing against the Iliad and Odysseus of the same Homer: affecting thereby the surname to be termed Homeromastix, Homer's whip.

It is the custom of all writers almost to interlace each other men's doings into their own: both because they may write things more certain, and also because their writings should be the more acceptable and pleasant unto the Reader. And as Falvius Albinus saith, this is one kind of fruit gotten by reading, that a man may imitate that which he liketh and alloweth in others: and such special points and sayings, as he is especially delighted and in love withal, by apt and fit derivation may wrest to serve his own turn and purpose.

Afranius also an excellent writer of comedies, in the answer that he made to them which laid to his charge that he had taken many things out of Menander: I confess, saith he, I have not only received and taken out of him, but also out of every other, as they seemed to have anything that made for my purpose: yea, out of Latin also have I excerpted and gathered whatsoever I thought myself could not do better. Quintillian giveth us in precept (which

Macrobius also advoucheth and laboreth to persuade), that we should imitate the little bees which do wander and fly abroad to seek their honey out of many flowers, and then dispose they in order whatsoever they bring home and couch the same in their combs and hives, and convert the diverse juice thereof with the breath of their mouths unto a most surpassing sweet honey, the pleasant relish whereof surmounteth all other. Neither may this seem new or strange, when we see that all authors, both Greek and Latin, do usually interlace their own works with other men's doings. For from Homer not only all poets have recourse even as all rivers from the ocean sea, but also the writers of all other matters: for we see that Strabo of Crete is altogether Homerical: and Cicero also, who for a great part delivereth and fetcheth his matter from Plato and Demosthenes, and translated into the Latin phrase the virtues of all the Greeks he liked. And so did Quintilia issue from Cicero, and all that have since his days studied eloquence and purity of the Latin tongue. Virgil also was not ashamed to translate into his works, thousands of Homer's verses, and lively to imitate his affections. So also borrowed he many things out of Hesiodus, Apollonius, and Theocritus. He took also much out of Latin writers, and when he misliked and disallowed of some, and was asked why he read them and noted anything out of them, he answered, *that he gathered precious stones out of the mire.*

Notwithstanding, I think it the part of a thankful mind, frankly to profess their names whom we do imitate, and of whom we have borrowed anything: for as Pliny saith, it is an honest thankfulness to confess by whom a man hath profited, and this recompense (as it were an hire) is payable unto the author by good right: lest otherwise we should seem to be unjust or deceitful in our dealings. Which thing also Thales Milesius hath taught us, for when as he being very old had devised a wonderful reason concerning the sun, and had taught the same unto Mandritus, a Philosopher of Cyrene, the said Mandritus, being greatly delighted with the novelty and strangeness of the invention (after great thanks first given to Thales therefore) willed him to choose what reward he would have in recompense of that so worthy a lesson: I shall think myself well and sufficiently recompensed (saith he to Mandritus) if wheresoever thou utterest this knowledge that thou has learned at my hands, thou do not arrogate and challenge the invention thereof to thyself, but declare and report me to be the inventor and deviser thereof, rather than any other man.

BOOK 1

OF THE ROYAL AND PRAISEWORTHY GOVERNMENT OF ONE SOLE
PRINCE. OF ORIGINAL CONSERVATION OF HUMAN SOCIETY. OF
PRESCRIBING POLITIC LAWS AND ORDINANCES. OF MAINTAINING
HUSBANDRY, TRADES OF MERCHANDISE, AND HANDYCRAFTSMEN.

I T HATH been a very old and published argument disputed
upon amongst excellent writers in Philosophy: whether it
were better to live well and safely to be governed by a good
Prince, and to obey him ruling in justice and equity; or else to live
in a free city and community established by good laws and
traditions. For unto some it seemeth more meet to obey one man
ruling justly and lawfully [rather] than many and almost infinite
persons (as for the most part it falleth out) unskillful in handling
affairs and matters of government. For it chanceth I know not how,
those several persons, who as it were workmen or porters we have
had in contempt, being linked or knit together in unity of mind,
the same afterwards hardly can we in assemblies reverence. For
they confirm this sentence by the testimony of Homer, who (in his
second Rhapsody) saith,

A matter cannot well handled be,
Where as commanders are many.

Moreover, unto this happeneth the imitation of nature, for as we see and behold one God the creator and fashioner of all things, by whose rule and commandment all things are governed: so seemeth it meet and convenient unto us all, to incline unto and regard the commandment of one most excellent Prince, and to obey the same. We see the sun in his nature, is as it were the only Lord of the day, and the moon to be the Lady of the night, whom we behold to rule and reign in the skies among the planets and stars, and the greater that their light is, the darker do they make the lesser stars.

But that we may descend unto lesser matters, are there not some brute beasts which live [as] subjects to the rule of some one king; they disdain not their obedience, nor to do their duties and commandments enjoined them, and fight as it were under a General. Who doubt that the bees have their King which governeth his people, and bringeth the other bees to do their duty and to gather honey. For there can be nothing sweeter or better to be wished unto mortal men, than to lead a private life under a good King or Prince without injury or ambition of the people. But because nature hath so ordained that Princes are not immortal or immutable persons, but some, being brought up very delicately, giving ear to flattering parasites, do for the most part prove worse and worse in their governing. Therefore, I judge that the life of a civil and well instituted common weale is to be thought far more safe, than of every Prince, for that is a continual and almost an immortal state of life. But this is finished in a small course by old age and death.

Very seldom it hath happened that a Prince governed and ruled still his common weale, in that mind as he did when he began first to take the government in hand. For of so great and almost infinite multitude of Caesars, which were all made worse by their continual reigns, only Vespasianus of all the Princes there were before his time was changed better and better, as Cornelius Tacitus maketh mention. For their beginnings were easy and gentle until such time as they had got unto themselves the love of their people, but when they had obtained their purpose, they made havoc of all things by their cruelty and lust. No fear of god, no religion could restrain them; neither ceased they to rage until they were subdued and subverted, yea, even by their own subjects.

Thales Milesius, who was called the chiefest of all the sages, being asked of a certain familiar friend of his what thing he had seen to be most difficult or hard in his lifetime: saith he, "a tyrant, an old man." And in good faith, not without a cause did he say so, for there is no rule or government exercised more hard then upon men, as Xenophon maketh mention.

Undoubtedly there is no brute beast so seditious or rebelling against his keeper or feeder, that he will not obey him, or refuse to yield his commodity unto him. But alas, man is grudging always at them which seek to have domination over him, deviseth deceits and inventeth new matters or causes of disobedience. One Prince which embraceth all virtues (or hath all good qualities in him) is not at all to be found living upon the earth. Some one is commended for his justice, some other for his fortitude or magnanimity, some other for his liberality or gentleness of nature: but when there are many in a common weale, every one of them hath some part of virtue and wisdom. Wherefore the citizens, being gathered together into one society, do make, as it were, one man, which with diversity of wit and memory doth excel, with many eyes seeth, with many hands worketh, and with almost infinite feet endeavoreth himself in his affairs. Xenophon, when he would praise the civil society of the Persians, affirmed that even their children among them did so learn justice, that they both attained unto good letters and also unto the studies of good arts and sciences.

It seemeth unto Plato a hard thing to be done, to persuade those citizens to justice, which were not from their tender infancy, as it were, trained up in the same. And undoubtedly, if the just and perfect volumes of the lawyers were extant and abroad to be handled, and that they were not so broken and mangled as they be, they would give us most clear and ample light—not only how to keep and preserve this civil society, but also they would teach us moral wisdom, and how to attain unto the use of the greatest affairs in a common weale.

Man is a creature far more fellowly and sociable than bees, ants, or cranes, and such kind of creatures which are fostered and nourished by flocks and do defend themselves by troops and companies. The first society is of the male and female for procreation's sake: which cannot be, except they be together: and scarce is the one withdrawn from the other except by the ordinance of nature: for the pledges of the younglings do so greatly cause mutual love, that they are careful to live together, and are affectioned towards their fruit as they be unto themselves. For it happeneth not unto man and woman as it doth almost unto all other living creatures, amongst whom the female sex do take on them the charge to feed and foster their young children, and for a small time it is that they stand in need of the mother's help. For we see that birds do bring up their young ones so long as they be unfeathered and not able to fly: but so soon as they perceive them able to use their wings, straightways they bring them forth of their nests and go before their young ones, which flicker round about them, until such time as with a stronger endeavor they be better able to shift for themselves, which when the old ones do see, they give those their young ones liberty, at their adventure to haunt the free scope of the air, neither have they afterwards any further care over them, or at any time these forth do acknowledge them as their own, but do take their flight to seek after the male bird, and give their endeavor unto a new increase or breed.

But man, when he seeth his children born and come into this world, is affected towards them with such love that he studieth or careth for nothing more than to get living for them and such large patrimony and inheritance, that for ever there be no lock of anything to them and their posterities. Of this did proceed and rise the plentifulness and fruitfulness of cities inhabited, because, when man and wife had edified for themselves a dwelling house and replenished the same with increase of children and nephews, they were driven to make other houses, because one house could not hold one lineage or offspring: and so they began to erect villages in the country and to establish society by means of many houses.

And when they did plainly see what commodity was in the society of man and woman: and how more easily and better very many lived together than a few: yea, more safe from the invasion of wild beasts: they began to join Lordship to Lordship, and lay Family to Family, and also to join in neighborhood for their own common utility. The first reason of the which instituted civil society, or established cities, was that they might live safely and that they might be defended from violence and assaults. For tranquility or peacableness was a guide of their life, to find our innumerable commodities. And it is credible that man's speech or language, wherein surely he doth excel other living creatures, was not distinct and severed before human society was first founded.

Certainly we have a common voice, as well as other living creatures have, which doth either specially demonstrate and show forth joy or sadness, either else sometimes desire, and sometimes fear, which is in us. But for to know and discern things by their proper names by plain and perfect speech, to finish or conclude as well our cogitations as our effects and meanings, that for certain could not be but invented by civil society of men. Moreover, the studies of virtues and disciplines, or rudiments of good arts and sciences, was not found out nor invented by men which lived in solitariness and of them which after the manner of savage beasts led their lives in the woods: but by the civil man, which was conversant in company of men which heard many things, which discussed many things, and by whom they were invented and first hand in use. For in such cities as were well instructed and ordered there were rewards bestowed on them which excelled in any manner of virtue and such as were also thereby preferred to high promotion and adorned or made famous, with praise and commendation for their excellence. For honor, as Cicero saith, doth foster and maintain arts and sciences, and we all are inflamed to endeavor ourselves for preferment and prerogative by praise and commendation in our travails. Finally, what excellent exploit so ever mortal men have by their study and diligence in this life put in ure, it either had first issue and original practice from the cities, or else took the use and grace thereof in the same cities.

Man which is brought up or trained in common society, differeth very much from him that liveth in rude cottage, either else in a hilly wilderness or wood: for this man seemeth to be born as it were unto cruelty, among wild and brute beasts, but the other seemeth to be born amongst men unto justice and humanity. For it is true that Aristotle saith,

> He is a beast and not a man which forsaketh civil society: and he that refuseth to be any part or member of a city, he must needs be a wicked and ungodly person.

For he shunneth the company of men because he would not be compelled to obey the laws and judgment, and [neither] to obey him that is a rightful ruler: then the which thing surely there can be nothing more pernicious or hurtful. For of all good civil order the chief thing is justice, which no doubt layeth the foundation and groundwork of human society and without the which there can be no civil congregation. For as the said Philosopher saith, as man is the best living creature of all others which liveth perfectly, so is he worst and naughtiest of all living creatures which is sequestered from the law and judgments.

The Laws of the Persians (as Xenophon writeth) do especially ordain the obedience due to justice, and in such manner even from their childhood (as we have said) the citizens did learn to desire nothing that was filthy or unlawful for man to do, which persuasion surely me thinketh is the best of all others. And if it might by any means be brought to pass, that all men might live instructed in this doctrine, we should be exonerated and discharged of a great part of our labor otherwise. For if every man would prescribe what were needful to be done, and being so linked and joined together were not affected or moved with covetousness, nor other perturbations of the mind: they should do rightwell. Ambition should not catch hold upon any man, covetousness should not snare any man, dissension or munity should not entrap any man, neither should envy circumvent any man, to withdraw him from the reason of that wherein truth and equity consisteth: neither should he pursue and seek for his private profit or inordinate pleasure, rather than a public weal, or that [which] reason, order, truth, and equity requireth.

Anacharsis, when he had heard say that Solon had given himself to the study of publishing Laws at Athens, exceedingly derided and scorned his industry and diligence, affirming that those laws should in time to come be like unto spider's webs, which did catch and keep fast the small flies, but were broken and burst in sunder of the great flies: which sentence also Solon himself would use and not without a cause: for oftentimes, in great cities (and wherein the studied of good arts and sciences do flourish), we see there are very many which live worse than as if they had been brought up in the woods and wild countries. Dion, in his books which are entitled, *Of the State of a Kingedome*, did say that weighty matters were far better handled by the counsel of a few persons than with a multitude and power of most strong and lusty young men: which indeed is ratified by the sentence of

Homer, where as he brought in Agamemnon as pertinent to his purpose, affirming that he could far more easily destroy the Trojan's common weale if he had ten such as Nestor or Ulysses were, than if he had so many such as Ajax and Achilles were, fighting stoutly and valiantly.

That state of a common weale wherein few do govern, differeth very little at all from the state of tyranny, for by their wealth and their riches the magistrates are chosen, and only wealth beareth sway. Neither doth this prescribe liberty or ends of virtue, but only how to get riches, which Cicero affirmeth: *are the subsidies of warfare and the ornaments of peace.* But the matter goes ill with the rich men, when no place is reserved for virtue, and the common people be as it were altogether brought under foot and subjection. And it comes to pass now and then that in some cities, only handycraftsmen and husbandmen do bear a sway, which, because they are more in number, they do decay those that be more noble of birth and calling, yea, and have such in derision and contempt which are zealous in any kind of virtue and learned in good arts or sciences. It may be brought to pass by fortune that such a city which is so governed may stand in safety and quietness for a certain time, but fortune frowning on them, it is soon perceived how hard a matter it will be to live well amongst such manner of men. For they that are brought up in fields or in shops void of experience in all things, and do bear authority with a servile mind, neither are they furthered or furnished with doctrine, nobleness of race, or with the experience of weighty affairs. And while they stand in fear of the nobler sort, they do all things either rashly without advisement or cruelly without measure: for every community either serves in obedience with humility or ruleth with great cruelty.

Furthermore, it seemeth contrary to equity, whereas the city cannot consist of nobles only, but far greater must be the rest of the multitude or community, that only the noble men should bear rule, and all the rest obey.

For tillage of ground and husbandry bringeth unto us natural nourishment, and merchandise doth bring unto us all other things necessary for our use: whereby it comes to pass that neither without husbandmen nor without merchants can civil society be amongst men.

They therefore are not to be exempted away from public offices, whose service is seen to be necessary in a common weale, lest they thinking themselves to be had in contempt, shrink away and withdraw themselves from the rulers and governors. For so often as the people of Rome did separate themselves from the senators, they were never without great peril and danger often renewed.

Surely the mean sort of men, which are neither too much abject or base, nor yet boast themselves in the wealth of their nobility, do far more modestly bear rule. But if it must needs be that either the nobility or community only should bear authority, I think it far more safely should the matter be handled by government of the nobles than of the commons: for seldom against comeliness or honesty doth be anything which seeth that by his doings he shall hazard the praise of his ancestors with himself, but he that being of himself base and obscure hath his ancestors far more obscure, seemeth to make unto himself a very small loss if sometimes he do anything amiss. And if their want no examples of rustical persons and men unknown which have fought valiantly for their country.

For we read, that some have been called from the plow, other some from the flock of sheep or other herds, which have obtained great victories unto the Romaines. But I am one of that number which account that to be the best common weale which is intermixed with all kind of people.

That is counted the best common weale wherein not every man that listeth or the more part do bear authority, at the beck and check of will, but that common weale wherein the Law only shall bear a sway: for equality of justice amongst citizens maketh a stable and firm society, which even then greatly flourisheth when as all things are judged and ordered with equal right and justice.

For it chanceth for the most part, that affections do trouble the judgments of men: some one, fear appalleth; some others, hatred; some hope; some other, awe and dread; and some other, ambition or covetousness compelleth to judge those things which are not only contrary to equity but also contrary to the mind of him which judgeth. For we see oftentimes the Judge moved with a certain affection, doth determine those things which within a short space after he would willingly alter and change.

Equality amongst citizens causeth concord, without the which, civil society is seen to be neither firm nor stable at all. For no force or strength can sufficiently prevail, no safeguard, no riches, no revenues can suffice those cities which are disquieted or troubled with intestine wars. And again also, neither shall that city be slender in power nor of small continuance which is environed and fortified with concord of the citizens. Therefore there must be great forecast had, that the citizens may live with equal justice and that some do not always bear rule, and that other some do not remain always as inferiors, for all society is unstable there, where all men do not live in indifferency of justice.

Man (for as much as he loveth and favoreth his own kin, is congregable or given to company, and sociable or given to fellowship more than other living creatures: and seeing no society can be firm or stable without justice) appeareth to be thereunto especially born, which he favoreth and is affected most unto.

And the first duty of justice is piety or godly zeal towards God: partaker of which virtue doubtless there is no living creature else seen to be, but only man. For man only doth acknowledge God, and him as the author and creator of the world, and workmaster of all things doth reverence and worship, by whom surely he acknowledgeth himself to be made partaker of reason, in whom he seeing that justice is all in all, it behooveth that he show himself a follower of justice, if he would have himself to be counted like unto himself.

It breedeth great dissension, where, amongst them which are found guilty in crime alike, some are grievously punished whereas other some escape untouched altogether: it should be otherwise if the offenses were not alike. For far more grievously is that governor or shipmaster to be punished, which overwhelmeth the same being laden with gold and silver, than he which hath lost or perished a ship laden with Sandelor Potter's clay, and yet either of these hath neglected his duty. For things of more value seem justly to require more diligence. For there can be no better persuasion in civil society than that which toucheth the freedom of the city, whereunto the mind of every citizen is to be directed, which surely shall be an easy matter to be done if in manner all men will hope and trust well that some time they may supply the function of a magistrate: for every man laboreth for renown, which when he shall see himself prevented of and that he is frustrated of hope, he is never at quiet in his mind, and either shall he be the more negligent in the common weale, or appear altogether evil affected toward the same. Hereupon do seditions grow amongst citizens, from hence do also rise factions and enmities, which things surely do weaken the state of a public weal: therefore a magistrate ought to have a determinate and prefixed time appointed for the government and exercise of his office. For, to bear authority continually in a free city is hateful: it must also be wisely foreseen that the citizens be found just among themselves, directing all their doings unto virtue, and being content with their own goods that they do not desire other men's.

Let there be no place for idle persons in a common weale, for surely by means of sloth and sluggishness they do commit all wickedness: whereupon true is that oracle of Marcus Cato, "By sloth and doing nothing at all, men learn to do evil, great and small." They do always envy at the painful travail of the good citizens, unto whom when they cannot be like, they labor with heart-burning and hatred how to weaken and disturb their estate. Such therefor as live idly must be excluded from public offices, because neither can they rule worthily and also do withdraw their duty from obedience. In which matters all civil society is contained.

Their opinion is not to be commended which say that by the fault or offense of the parents, their posterity should be forever excluded out of the public weale, for in so doing they shall despair altogether of felicity when they see that all hope of pardon is debarred: and that they cannot redeem themselves by any virtue or worthiness. For it oftentimes chanceth that their minds are most ready and prone to innovation, and desperation sometime is turned into mighty courage: for they which are in any extremity do easily take hold upon the sentence of the most learned poet Maro, "Una salus victis, nullam sperare salutem." It is only counted a safety unto those which be vanquished or convinced, not to hope for any safety at all.

Of all things, (as Cicero writeth) whereof there is any commodity to be gotten, nothing can be better or more commodious than husbandry or tillage of ground. Than this, nothing is more plentiful, nothing sweeter, neither yet more worthy for the state of a freeman in a common weale: for only husbandry is such as unto whom gentlemen and others ought to set to their hands, both for that sustenance unto our life, (forasmuch as without the same we cannot live) and again because it yields a most honest gain without deceit or lying.

Surely young men are made strong with the exercise of tillage of the ground, and be far more healthy than such as are trained up in cities, where as they, using sleep and lusts of the body, are enfeebled and unhealthy.

It is not therefore to be marveled, if the Romans brought forth young men hardened in the fields, when they conquered the whole world, not by idleness and sloth, but with strength and fortitude.

But we in these days do shun the trade of husbandry as filthy lucre, yea, and have the husbandmen in derision, and do despise them as slaves or bondmen, and such as are born to perpetual drudgings, and do esteem brokers, peddlers, cooks, and cobblers more than we do of a good husbandmen, whose industry we then do say exceedeth the industry of all other workmen, when the common people ready to starve for hunger earnestly craveth their help and nourishment, and when they, being hunger-starved and pinched with famine, becometh unruly and past all fear. For husbandry only yields unto nourishment, it helpeth and furthereth building, and almost findeth sufficiency also of apparel: only the husbandman is a breeder of cattle: which thing was of such estimation among the ancient people that Cato being demanded, in what thing a man might be quickly made rich: if (saith he) a man feed well. And being again demanded what thing else? (saith he) if he feed well. By the which answer he showeth us, that even a mean diligence of the master in feeding his cattle exceeds the other profits. For indeed there is no art or science nor any industry of men sooner maketh a man rich than husbandry.

Hesiodus and Homer did more allow of the instruments and necessaries pertaining to husbandry and of husbandmen than of warriors or warlike affairs: for the one promiseth unto men life and felicity, the other death and misery.

Good householders ought to take account of their servants and families' idleness, rather than of their business: and the most learned of the ancient fathers judged that there was nothing more odious and hateful than sloth and drowsiness of the mind: wherefore, before they should eat their meat, they called the young men and servants to the table, and took account of them what duty or what business they had done that day: and before them only they set meat: whose diligence they liked and allowed, and those they thrust out of the place accustomed to sup in, which by their sloth and sluggishness had done nothing: and commanded that they should labor hard in some dutiful business to earn their own food. Let those take upon them this charge which especially in a common weale do bear rule: to see that young men do apply their minds unto the study of good arts of sciences. For in every free city, there ought to be a special care for the maintenance of good arts and sciences. For Plato said: "Blessed are those common weale which of wise and learned men are governed."

Or at the least (seeing we all cannot prove learned) wherein merchandise, seafaring trade, and other sciences profitable unto civil society were frequented and used.

Every man ought to labor as much as he may, to profit himself, his family, and other citizens. For amongst those most straight laws which Draco made, there was especially one, that, they which were condemned for idleness, should be punished with death.

Diodorus writeth that there was a law among the Egyptians, whereby all men were compelled to declare their names unto their rulers and to show by what art or by what manner of gain they lived. And if any man lied or lived by unjust lucre or gain, the same was adjudged to die: and truly not without a cause: for those that be idle and slothful young men are the poison of the city: they are apt and prove to lust and pleasure, they do envy those that be good, they covet and desire other men's goods, and finally the prove seditious and troublous men, insomuch as the greatest troubles rise upon them.

Marcus Cato wrote very well in his books of Manners, that man's life was as iron, which if a man do exercise and put in use, is in wearing made bright, but being unexercised and not put in use, is with rust consumed and cankered. So men with honest exercise are in like case tried and worn, and if they be not exercised, sloth and drowsiness doth bring to them more detriment and damage than diligence or painstaking doth good.

For very well doth Cato touch the same in his Oration made at Numantia to the horsemen, saying: "You soldiers, consider in your minds if you shall do any thing well by labor or travail, the labor and travail doth quickly depart, but the good that you do in the same labor and travail, still doth remain forever: but if you take any pleasure in doing evil, the pleasure quickly departeth, but the evil that you do, remaineth forever." Which sentences declare that there is nothing worse than idleness, neither anything more praiseworthy than industry and travail. Merchants and handycraftsmen are to be favored, which with their labor and industry get their living: for, merchants are necessary which do carry away from us such things as we have superfluous or too much store of, and by exchange and sales of their commodities do bring us those things which shall be necessary for us.

The custom of the Belgians and low countrymen doth seem to me very allowable, because they will not suffer merchants to come and traffic with them which shall bring unto them those things that may cause them to be effeminately minded. For it chanceth in our times that the provocations of venery and lusts, as enticements to vain pleasures, on every side are brought us from the furthest part of the ocean sea. Certainly such manner of navigation or traffic cannot be necessary, and as I judge must needs be less commendable, but only that which make the exchange with superfluous things for such kind of commodity, as may be most for our profit.

A certain Laconian did say (as it is reported) that there is an end or measure to be prescribed unto lucre or gain, for and in consideration of the diverse chances of fortune: lest he that in a small moment of time the merchant do loose and let slip that which in all his lifetime he hath gained, and be compelled of necessity to consume and waste the same in expenses, which thing undoubtedly cannot come to pass without reproach and dishonesty, although the party be nothing faulty.

Therefore, to the end that merchants may live without such reproach, let them prescribe unto themselves a measure and end in their covetous attempts, lest they be compelled to suffer poverty in their old age, with derision also.

And yet notwithstanding, Socrates judgeth them that buy of those great merchants to the intent to sell the same again, to be worthy of dispraise, except by weakness of age or by reason of their unhealthfulness of body they cannot put in practice any other kind of trade to live upon.

The law of Solon is praised especially wherein he ordained that, that child was not bound unto his father in any necessary duty of life, of whom he had received no art, science, or trade to get his living withal.

Handycraftsmen or workmen which provide those things that are profitable unto us, and without whom we may less commodiously live, are not only to be born withal: but also are to be taken and reputed amongst the most honest citizens. Smiths, founders, carvers, engravers, printers, potters, glassiers, shoemakers, couriers, tailors, weavers, joiners, masons, clothiers, pargeters, roughmasons, ironmongers, and very many other suck like faculties are to be admitted, partly because they provide such things as be necessary, partly because they make their city more noble with diverse ornaments.

The Lacedemonians, to the end they might withdraw their citizens from all filthy gain, and provoke them unto husbandry, hunting, and warfare, did caste out of their city as well their gold as their silver: counting it a pestilence or plague unto the citizens, and ordained to be made a certain coin of iron which was more weighty, to the end they might be extruded and sequestered from all company of their neighbors, and live without the trading to or with any foreign countries. They which trade in merchandise with modest and do take no usury (which thing Marcus Cato declared was the next point to a murderer) for to one that demanded of him, what it seemed unto him, to be an usurer, he answered, what it is to kill a man. And they which do not lie, neither deceive others with perjury or lying, I deem them worthy to be enriched with the benefits of a common weale.

Workmen given to filthy gain and which are the ministers of pleasures, and do provide for the provocations of gluttony and lechery, are not only not to be admitted into a common weale, but also to be thrust out of a city: for with their tipping houses and places of riot they do [bring] hurt unto many and profit to no man.

And those that exercise or use light arts and faculties, which riseth no profit, are to be neglected and had in contempt and rather to be derided than esteemed or rewarded.

The first respect or regard of giving our voices is to be had of honesty and virtue. And the second of liberal sciences which in a city bring with them most plentiful profit. The third consideration is to be had of nobility, for they whose ancestors have flourished famous with some kind of praise, their children and posterity are not to be neglected, except by their reproach or ignominy they do darken and blemish the praise and commendation of their ancestors. And the fourth consideration ought to be had of them which profit the citizens by trade of merchandise, workmanship, and industry, making the city thereby more wealthy and renowned.

Vulcane, who was most skillful in the art of astronomy and which was also the successor of Mercury in the kingdom, did invent the mines of silver, gold, and iron. The Grecians hold opinion that he first made and devised the fire tongs of brass or copper, and other necessaries touching husbandry. And they say that in the art of war he could do very much: and that he was made lame by reason of a wound which he received in his foot: he also held opinion that the planets and stars were fiery, and that all things were made and created of fire.

It shall therefore behoove them which bear rule in a common weale, to be careful that there want no devisers or chief workmasters in a city: for when the sacred or public buildings are by evil measure and proportion framed, that ministereth occasion to strangers to think that the chief princes and rulers of that common weale are clean void of elegancy: but private men's houses being evil timbered, unhandsomely severed with windows and lights, and beautified uncomely, are for habitation nothing handsome and expedient. Let the chief master of the work therefore respect and look well to the form and fashion of houses in the city and to the commodity of the building and houses, in time of peace and quietness: but in time of wars for an architect or chief deviser of works shall stand in so good steed for engines, guns, and other munitions, that he cannot but be worthy of great preferment, honor, and public offices: for we read of some cities that have been delivered from the siege of their enemies, only by the skillful diligence of the chief deviser or workmaster.

Amongst other spectacles which throughout all the world are praised, the city of Thebes in Egypt was counted for the greatness thereof, for the walls and for building, most worthiest of admiration: for it had city gates by situation distinct and severed one from another, with notable and artificial workmanship, whereupon it had so glorious a name and was of such excellency that all the whole province there was called by the name of the citizens of Thebes: and yet the same was subverted before the Empire of Rome.

The brick walls of Babylon which Semiramis builded, contained compass 385 furlongs in height: between the towers 50 cubits, and in breadth 30 foot.

The art of painting showeth in itself great erudition and learning, and much resembleth poetry. For Sextus Empiricus (after the opinion of Symonides the poet) said that a picture is a still or silent poesie, ant the poesie to be a talking picture: and certainly it is an art of great wisdom and doth touch near unto divine knowledge so to conceive in mind the diverse forms of living creatures and other things, so to express them with pencil an diverse colors that there seems nothing wanting unto them but life and breath.

For we read that an oxe did low at the beholding of a certain pictured oxe: and that not a few have been deceived with the sight of grapes pictured. And that birds have also been stirred up to rejoice at the painted proportion or similitude of their kind.

For a picture hath not only a grace with it, and giveth wonderful delectation: but also reserveth the memory of things that are done and past, and showeth perpetually before our eyes the by-story of things that are done. And moreover, in reading of painted stories wherein notable exploits are expressed, we are excited unto the studies of praise and to the endeavor of accomplishing weighty and great matters. Wherefore it shall not be feared lest that the hands of young men be stained or spotted with colors, seeing painting cometh nearest unto learning itself.

Julius Caesar, being sent as Ouestor or Treasurer into Spain, when he came to Gades, marking well and beholding the image of Alexander the Great in the Temple of Hercules, sighed, and as it were bewailed his own sloth and negligence, that as yet in those years of his he had not done anything worthy praise: whereas Alexander before he attained to that age, had conquered the greatest part of the world.

He required of the Senate that he might have free liberty to ease himself of those affairs: and being pricked forward with memorial of such like praise, within a small time he excelled and surmounted the deeds and prowess of Alexander of Macedon. Cato Censorius seemed scarce quiet in mind because there was no image erected for him: and unto one that demanded him why he had not his picture or image as well as a great sort of others, he answered: "I had rather that good men should muse and doubt, why I have it not, than (which is worse) to murmur in their minds, why I should have it."

FINIS.

BOOK 2

OF CAREFUL REGARD FOR THE SUPPORT OF LEARNING, THE NECESSARY UTILITY OF LIBERAL ARTS AND SCIENCES, AND EXAMPLES PERSUADING TO THE USE OF OTHER EXERCISES CORPORAL PROFITABLE TO A WEALE PUBLIC.

T HE KINGS of Egypt far more esteemed the praise of good disciplines and sciences than of warfare. And therefore they all with a wonderful diligence bent themselves to the studies of wisdom; neither did any of them think himself able or sufficient enough to bear rule, unless he surmounted and excelled the residue in some kind of doctrine or learning, and employed his whole endeavor to the furtherance and profiting of many others.

With this industry, Ptolomeus being incited, [then] furnished and made that famous library at Alexandria, to the end he might thereby sow the seed of wisdom unto his posterity, and profit both the citizens and also strangers.

He also instituted plays unto the Muses and unto Apollo, and ordained unto poets and orators at their disputations, as unto champions in their combats, great rewards and high dignities, that they might the more diligently take pains in the studies and exercises of learning.

Learning (doubtless) was most ancient among the Egyptians, whose priests which were conversant about their kings and rulers, were accounted the first of all others that were notable in the mathematical sciences; and unto them also did resort thick and threefold, scholars out of all nations of the world to learn: neither was any man though sufficiently learned, which was not skillful in the Egyptian lore or discipline, to the attaining whereof (as Diodorus Siculus maketh mention) Orpheus Musaeus, Melampus, Daedalus, Homerus, Lycurgus, Solon, Pythagoras, Plato, Eudoxus, Democritus, Euripedes, and many others went thither, who have made famous all disciplines of all other nations.

I deem it best first and especially that all men (if it were possible) should be learned. Neither am I of their opinion which say that learning is the plague and destruction of wit and memory, amongst whom was Plato, who affirmed that the use of letters was a hindrance unto memory, because those things (which we have laid up in writing) we (as it were) cease to keep in memory: even as those things which we have laid up in strong chests, under lock and key, we think to be sure enough, and take no more care there for. Notwithstanding, amongst all the devices of men, I doubt whether ever anything were devised or uttered more excellent: for it seemeth a thing strange and miraculous how in a few notes or letters, so infinite speeches of men and innumerable words and sentences should be comprised and comprehended: for all kind of doctrine and learning should be mortal and subject unto decay, yea, the acts and gests of men should be soon buried in oblivion, if they were not registered and reserved in monuments of learning: which have been so highly accounted of, that many, both people and most excellent personages, do challenge to themselves the invention thereof.

Those letters therefore do I deem not only to be throughly learned: but also scarcely can I think any man in a free city can or may deserve the name of a witty citizen without the knowledge of learning: for how without learning can we attain not only unto the high knowledge of liberal sciences, but also thereby learn many small arts or faculties; neither can merchandise itself or husbandry be [of] sufficient safety without them: for these do keep the memory of things past, they instruct posterity: they annex and compare things done and past unto things yet to come, and do keep a perpetual reckoning of all our whole life.

The best way here in to be done therefore is to train young children hereunto before they apply any other matters: if in time to come we desire to have them prove men, or to be reputed and taken in the number of citizens: for surely the Greek proverb is:

> *A man void of skill and wanting learned lore,*
> *To a tree unprofitable, compared is evermore.*

Governors therefore of common weale ought to be careful and diligently to foresee that for every liberal art or good learning, there may be assigned the best schoolmasters to be maintained with a public stipend, which may teach openly: for every private person cannot maintain living for their children, and recompense their schoolmasters with convenient stipend and ordinary salary. And especially let the schoolmasters teaching grammar be excellent and notable, yea, not only in learning but in manners also most approved: for it is most dangerous, as it is spoken in the Proverb, *to betake a sheep into the custody of a wolf.* And to find him whom thou puttest in trust as schoolmaster to thy children, a corrupter and marrer of them: for the vices wherewith the children at that age are polluted, do either remain perpetually or else with great difficulty are they withdrawn from them.

The Romans so greatly esteemed grammar that by decree they ordained the same to be taught with a common salary in the open streets or highways, by means whereof it was called long time the common science: many affirm that this art was first devised and invented at Memphis, a city in Egypt.

Pythagoras, the Prince of Italian Philosophy (whom Plato doth in all points for most part imitate) thinketh the sciences mathematical to be most necessary for the civil man: in vain (as he judgeth) shall a man study philosophy, which hath not tasted of the same, not (as they say) superficially, but even throughly and effectually.

Lucius Columella would have every day to be observed by the rules of astronomy, both for profit in husbandry, and again, for the avoiding of manifold dangers whereof we may be warned to take heed by them that be skillful.

Anaximander Milesius forewarned the Lacedaemonians that they should look well to their city and houses: for he foresaw by this science that there was an earthquake at hand, which thing doubtless came so to pass: and a great part of that city and of the hill Taygetus fell flat to the ground.

So Hyppocrates did foreshow a plague or pestilence which should come from the Illyrians, and dispersed his scholars round about the cities of Greece, to succor and relieve them that should be diseased.

Pericles, General of the Athenians, when as his host was astonied at the eclipse of the sun and ready to yield victory to their enemies, whom they thought the gods more favored, delivered them from their perplexity, disclosing the cause namely that it was the natural order of the sun, and that it came not to pass by any displeasure of god or any unnatural event.

In the discipline or doctrine of astronomy and in other sciences mathematical, Publius Nigidius did very greatly excel among the Romaines: to whom was attributed for a surname, Potter, by reason of his excellent device and invention of that knowledge: for when it was proposed and argued, why two twins both born at one birth should have diversity of destiny, seeing they were both begotten and born under one planet, and defending his art, denied that they could not be, by reason of the swift moving of celestial orbs, showing the same by this means, he stirred about the whel that bare about the potter's clay with great force, and upon the same did cast two drops of ink, and after a pause made from turning the wheel, the drops were found a good way sonder, in the uttermost parts of the wheel: how now (saith he) can they think that twins be a like destined and born under one planet, when as the heavens are moved and whirled with so swift moving and turning: seeing the wheel of a potter being turned about with a small course doth manifest before your eyes, the two drops of ink at one time to be shaken and sprinkled into two several places: surely this device was so well liked of the audience, that it yielded unto the author the palm and victory of the disputation and a perpetual surname.

Lycurgus did so allow and esteem the science of music, that he affirmed the same to be given unto men by nature to the more easy bearing and toleration of their labors and travails: and he ordained the use of playing on the shalms in warfare, whereupon they should play both at their marching forwards and at their retire also: and so stir up and encourage the minds of the soldiers that even the most cowardly person being pricked forth with the sounds thereof, did sometimes prove the most valiant and achieved the victory for their country. The people of Creta also, when they were about to assault their enemies, were excited and encouraged to fight by the noise of the harp. The Argiues with shalms as the Latins with trumpets, and the Frenchmen with cornets, were encouraged and animated.

Tymotheus, the most excellent musician, when he was disposed to advance himself any time before Alexander the king, tuned his instruments so cunningly and musically that the king, having mind of none other thing but that only and being therewith pierced and penetrated to the heart, as it were, by some divine admiration would straight lay hand on his weapon and take thereby occasion to overcome his enemies.

Music in a free city is to be allowed, yea, although it brought no other thing else than pleasure and delight: for we cannot always be busied in affairs: and this kind of oblectation even in our business and dealings is most honest: for as Cicero saith very well: "It is the part of a free man sometimes to do nothing, and to withdraw his wearied mind from long care otherwise." Which thing especially music bringeth to pass, making us thereby to forget our labors, travails, and miseries.

Plato devised three sorts of music. The one he said was manifest, consisting only in the voice, as we see is used when men sing. The second as well with the voice as with the hand, as when with the striking upon the strings we use to sing to the instruments. The third (saith he) is only finished with the hands and fingers, as when the voice being silent and still, we strike and play upon an instrument.

Pythagoras thinketh that music was not the invention of men but of the first workmaster of the universal world, which made the celestial orbs to yield and make a certain harmony in their distinct motions, whereout proceedeth the first invention of human music: which music doubtless is profitable unto a civil person, and doth not only delight the mind but also nourish the wit, making men more prompt and courageous, not only in warlike affairs but also to achieve every weighty matter.

And moreover we read of Paeon and diverse other physicians, whose patients almost despairing of recovery, have been healed and recovered by the delights and pleasures taken in music, and that certain men have been brought to their right wits again by the same mean.

It we will have any regard of the health of our bodies and tranquility of life, which without prosperous health can scarcely be had, we shall confess that physic is the most excellent and necessary art pertaining unto mortal men. For as Cornelius Celsus maketh mention, who hath written most excellent books of this discipline: husbandry affordeth nourishment to our bodies when they be healthful, and physic promiseth health unto persons diseased: and therefore we ought to render thanks to the living god, who hath granted us life: next of all unto the physician who doth conserve the same unto us, and maketh health fuller and of longer continuance. For to prove that this art of all other sciences is most ancient, the best learned Greek authors do testify: for the inventor hereof was Apis the son of Phoroneus, and Pytho king of Egypt.

The ancient writers divided physic into three parties: the one to consist in diet, another in remedies or medicines, and the third in artificial cure of the hand: and unto this part did the inventions of Alcmaeon Crotoniata, scholar to Pythagoras the physician, much help, who, searching every member of man's body and cutting up all and every joint and inward article of all the vital parts, was the first that devised and invented the dissection or anatomy of man's body.

If medicine for the body be necessary in a good common weale, for the sundry kinds of diseases which chanceth daily unto mortal men, so then with strong and sound bodies we may live well: how much more necessary shall the physic of the soul and mind be, without the which the bodies themselves cannot be in good health or liking? For man is subject unto many diseases, by reason of the diverse kinds of meats whereof he feedeth, as Homer saith: yet notwithstanding the diseases of the mind are not fewer than the diseases of the body, and wherewith we be far more vexed and endangered: what disease seemeth anger to be, wherewith when we be throughly chafed, little or nothing do we differ from made and furious frantic persons? What disease seemeth covetousness to be? Wherewith when we be throughly inflamed, we cannot be grateful unto our own country, not to our parents nor children, neither yet unto ourselves: What doth fear? What doth trembling? What doth sloth and sluggishness work and bring to pass in us? And other perturbations of the mind innumerable, which when they seize upon us, we are not only in mind but also in body disquieted: but the medicine or physic for the mind is specially eloquence, which by the reasons and arguments of philosophy represseth or keepeth under such persons as would be too much puffed up with vices, lifting up those that are cast down and making very dastards to become valiant persons: for what other force or power can there be better than by the force of eloquence, to bridle the raging and furious common people, when their courage faileth them for fear, and to stir them afresh to valiance.

Ancient writers say that eloquence was the lady and mistress of matters, neither is it only accounted profitable in peace and quietness, but also in wars and tumults excelleth all other strength and force: which thing to be true Pyrrhus king of the Epirotes affirmed. For when he did mak wars in Italy, he retained as his companion of his exploits, Cyneas the Thessalian, as an orator and disciple of Demosthenes, using his help and service at each pitch most earnestly: for unto the cities which he could not subdue by force and armor, he sent Cyneas his orator: which cities for the most part he persuaded to surrender, even as he desired:

insomuch that Pyrrhus used oftentimes to say that more cities were won and brought under his power and subjection by the eloquence of Cyneas than were by himself vanquished by force of arms.

The art of oratory consisteth in three sorts of causes, whereof the first containeth persuasion and dissuasion: for what things soever are in a common weale advised or deliberated upon, they have need of persuasion and dissuasion, to the intent the truth may be bolted out: wherefore an orator, that is to say a good man, skillful and flowing in utterance, shall persuade such things as shall be thought profitable, lest the people slide or fall away by a sinister and false opinion, and allow well of that which within a little space after they shall either be compelled to alter and change, or, with repentant minds, bear and suffer the same impatiently. The second is called the kind demonstrative, consisting either in praise or dispraise: and the third kind is that which in judgments is exercised, and this falleth out into accusation and defense.

But many cities nowadays are nestled in an ill error, because either lawyers are altogether ignorant of pleading causes, or rather because light disposed babblers, as the ancient writers did call them, do plead and handle matters only for lucre sake, babblingly, and thereupon delaying suits make the same to hang in strife and variance very long, which thing in cities is very dangerous: for private grudges breedeth discord among citizens.

Among the Venetians, whose common weale is for justice, government, wealth, and nobility of the citizens, accounted not only throughout all Italy but also throughout all the world, most famous and excellent: the most learned persons of all others, in the art of oratory, and such as become of a noble race, do pleas and handle their causes: by which means through continual exercise, they do attain to that perfection that very many of them prove cunning and eloquent men in their common weale.

Poets are to be maintained in a city, and to be made famous as well with honor as with praise: which persons surely ought to be most cherished and welcomed unto all men, as well for the rarity of them (for nothing in all ages of man can be sound more rare than a good poet) as also for the abundance of their wit and their divine nature; neither shall poets be exiled from a good city, whatsoever Plato shall say, seeing they are well known to be very profitable unto their country. For what learning hath grammar in it contained without the pertraction of poets? The elegancy or fineness of words, the propriety of the tongue, the sweet translations or metaphors, the liberty of speech and sentences, which do beautify the orations, as it were, with certain stars— were they not invented only by poets and aptly placed and distinguished by them, in their rightful places?

Socrates the Philosopher was wont to say, it small fancied or liked him to behold the secrets of nature, and to neglect the reason and order of man's life: for what profiteth it us to search out certain hidden secrets of nature, to measure the stars and skies in our minds, if we know not ourselves and [if we] neglect the reason or order which ought to govern our appetite, and whereby we differ from brute beasts.

What may be more vile or filthy than to see a man that is well learned to be with lust inflamed, furious, or angry, covetous, or unsatiable without measure insomuch the more he hath, the more he seems to lack. Surely unto such a man that happeneth, which Thales the philosopher, one of the seven sages happened: for he on a time in the night season walking abroad did behold the heavens very earnestly, by means whereof he fell into a ditch or pit that was in his way where he went, whereat he cried out: a certain old wife looking out at her window, and hearing him cry, asked him what he went about to do, that he so fell into the pit: whereupon he answered, that his meaning was to behold the heavenly planets: but the old woman smiling said, *thou seest not those things which are before thine eyes, and yet wilt thou seek to know heavenly matters?*

The Oracle at Delphos (which they say was fixed before the doors of the Temple) ought to be prefixed before all men's eyes which desire to be right wise: which is *Know thyself*: for he knoweth not himself which doth not know how to use the virtue of his mind, which is broken or shaken with fear, which doth advance himself beyond measure in rejoicing, who is inflamed with covetousness, tormented with lusts: against which evils, philosophy armeth us, and doth not only pluck up the roots but also every little string or fiber of perturbations. To this philosophy will every good citizen endeavor himself that desireth to profit not only himself and his, but his native country also.

Philosophy teacheth us that throughly that justice is it which containeth and keepeth together human society: without the which there can neither city neither yet any house be rightly governed: for she persuadeth us to use and enjoy our own right, and not to injure any man, to live content with our own goods and to abstain not only our hands but also our eyes from other men's goods.

The knowledge of Philosophy is not only pleasant unto citizens but also to kings, princes, and governors, and doth much avail in the enterprise of great or weighty matters: for Philip of Macedonia, when news was brought him that his son Alexander was born, he directed his letters unto Aristotle, saying: that he gave hearty thanks to the gods, not only for that he had a son born, but because it was his fortune to be born in the time of Aristotle, of whom undoubtedly he hoped he should instructed, and that he should prove a son both worthy for him and the succession of his crown: and therefore so soon as this his son could speak, he gave charge that he should be brought up at the beck or commandment of Aristotle, committing him in his lusty green age unto his charge to be further trained in disciplines and learning: and when his master Aristotle, by reason of sickness, could not well attend and follow him in his wars, he resigned his roam unto Calysthenes his scholar, that he might ever be at hand and ready with the king and further him in the studies of Philosophy.

Pericles, who had done so many famous exploits amongst the Athenians, had for his schoolmaster, Anaxagoras, whose precepts he is reported very often to have put in use, not only in civil and domestical, but also in foreign and warlike affairs, wherein he being studiously bent to take pains and hearing that Anaxagoras being weary of his long life, went about the famish himself to death, with all expedition, came to him, and, as a petitioner with prayer and tears desired him, that if he had no mind or joy to live unto himself: that yet at least he would live for Pericles sake, whose conference and counsel in matters tending to the common weale, he greatly wished to have.

Julius Caesar was a man most exquisite in all kind of learning, and enriched all the best learned men in his time with rewards and promotions: by whose example also, Octavius Augustus retained Athenodorus as his schoolmaster in Philosophy, a man as learned as any in his time.

The Frenchmen, which are called Celtae, affirm that they whom they called in their mother tongue *Druids*, were the first inventors of Philosophy: for these persons, inhabiting the woods, not only in contemplation but also in life, showed themselves precise philosophers, and disputed many things of virtue and of the immortal God, very godly: and held opinion, that death was no other thing than a certain flitting unto a better and more lasting life: who, being induced with that persuasion, fought valiantly and without fear against their enemies, thinking that man altogether a dastard and fool which feared death: seeing even forthwith they should by death pass into a far better life.

We have already told that first especially civil man must labor to furnish his mind with disciplines and studies of good arts: for the excellency of the mind doth not only help the body, but also maketh it most ready to the achieving of all and every great labor: for there can no body be strong and healthy enough, when the mind languisheth: for in the wars we do often see that some little men and small of stature do fight with a good courage, and those which are bigger to be very cowards: and therefore it is better to help and fortify the mind with virtue and wisdom, if we desire to have the right strength of the body.

The exercise of men's body is altogether counted necessary: for sloth doth dull the body and maketh men given to too much tenderness, but industry or labor doth strengthen the body, and maketh men more lusty and strong.

For the Lacedaemonians nourished their children in the country and used to wrestle naked, to the end they might accustom themselves the better to endure travel and labors. They lodged abroad under the open air, as well in time of cold as in time of heat, and hardened themselves in the dust, in running, shooting, wrestling, casting, and leaping. To set before valiant persons and stout warriors, the sweet delights of boys and girls, seems to me no other thing than to weaken the strength and to have all virtue in contempt and derision. Let children therefor be so exercised that they may accustom themselves to take pains and labor, but yet not in outrageous savageness: for as industry and honest exercise doth strengthen the body and make it more apt unto labor and travail: so too much exercise and continual travel doth break, cut off, and shorten a man's days with untimely old age. Aristotle witnesseth that with such kind of toil, the growth of the body is hindered and the members wrenched and disfashioned. Celsus saith that we see many times men of great toil and labor to become, in the end, most crooked and benumbed in their members.

Julius Caesar commanded that young warriors should not be trained or taught, neither in the school nor by masters of defense, but at home in their dwelling houses, by the horsemen and senators, skillful in feats of arms, in wrestling, running, casting of the ball: in which practices, he liked well to have them exercised, yea, he thought it would do them much good to be inured in swimming, leaping, skirmishing, and making a show of a right battle in deed: for they that accustom themselves to such exercises come more cheerfully and with better courage to the wars, and are both in body and mind stronger.

Epaminondas, the most worthy captain of the Tebanes, inured himself much with wrestling, not so much to get a corporal strength as for the agility and nimbleness of his body: also Plato the greatest of all philosophers exercised wrestling with Aristo Argiuus, by reason whereof it is said that for the notable habit of his bady, he was called Plato: for afore he was called Aristocles, after the name of his grandsire.

The Lacedaemonians commanded their women to wrestle among them, and joined in marriage, the man [as] conqueror with the woman [as] conqueress together: [to the end] the issue afterward coming of strong and lusty parents, should be likewise stronger than others: but this custom is altogether refused and rejected. Let women therefore keep themselves at home and apply their housewifely affairs, whom nature hath made and ordained weak and fearful persons, that by means of fear and awe they might be the fitter and apter to keep home.

Let first the wit of a child be nourished and trained unto wisdom if it may be: which of all other things is the best and chiefest: let him be exercised in body but yet so as he hinder not thereby the gifts and dexterity of his wit: for it is hard for a child to be exercised in body and mind together at one time, whereof there would be diligent consideration and reason had: for they need bodily exercise but a small while, lest they should be therewith too much delighted: for they are made thereby more dull of capacity and scarcely know how to provide for themselves: as we read of Milo Crotoniates, of whom it is reported that he did all things beyond the strength and ability of man, and often winning the best game and victory, was crowned: and killing an oxe with one blow of his fist, sacrificed him, but at length, trusting too much to his strength, he came to a most miserable death and doleful end: for espying a tree where into wedges were driven, but not yet clove asunder, and laughing at the sloth of them that had left the same tree, in that case so remaining he went about to tear it asunder with his hands, but when the wedges were loosed and fallen out, and that the tree came together again to his proper nature, he was taken fast by the arms in that desert and unable to help out himself, was devoured of wild beasts and fowls of the air.

Poldyamas, another famous champion, entering on a time into a certain cave, and willing to sit down, his froward fortune was such that the upper part of the cave over them opened wide and fell down upon them. Polydamas therefore going about with his arms and shoulders, to bear up the weight, all his companions, leaving him distressed, fled away, and he thereby fondly enforced to make for himself his grave there not without the great derision of all the company.

Secundi libri.

FINIS.

Book 3

OF THE ELECTION AND CHOICE OF MAGISTRATES IN A COMMON WEALE. OF MORAL EXAMPLES IN FURTHERING THEIR OFFICES AND DUTIES IN SEVERAL. OF DISCUSSING AND REDRESSING CAUSES IN VARIANCE. OF REFORMING ENORMITIES AND CONTROVERSIES. OF NEEDFUL ORDINANCES. OF ACCUSTOMED WATCHES FOR DEFECT AND SAFEGUARD OF THE CITY OR COUNTRY. OF CAREFUL PROVISION FOR CORN AND VICTUALS, NEEDFUL AS WELL IN PEACE AS IN WARS FOR THE PUBLIC SUSTENATION.

A LL GOVERNANCE of a common weale consisteth in the description and choice of magistrates, without whose authority, wisdom, and diligence a city cannot flourish nor be. For amongst people that live in freedom, there is nothing well done without magistrates: for even as a ship without a pilot can never be brought into the haven of tranquility, and as an host of men, without a captain, is always in great danger and scarcely ever winneth the victory: in like manner, evil society seemeth to be objected and laid open unto fortune: neither can be in any part quiet or fortunate, except (by the authority and counsel of the magistrates) it be governed. And yet notwithstanding, multitude of magistrates troubleth and perturbeth the order of a city. For as in seafaring and warlike business, regard must be had that there be but few commanders and many obeyers: so also judge I it meet and requisite to be observed in the state of a common weale.

Ancient writers commend the Massilians whose common weale for order sake and equity they prefer before others: for they had senators, in number (as Strabo maketh mention) 600, of whom 15 every year by turns bore greatest authority: and of those 15, also 3 were appointed to decide laws and matters in controversy, and these few only governed the civil society very well; but in time of wars and uproars, these Massilians did choose such Generals and Princes as were sufficient and well able to take some weighty charge of wars in hand: for very many physicians being brought unto one sick person do rather strive amongst themselves by way of vain ostentation than minister those things which may heal or remedy the patient. And diverse counsels or opinions in greatest dangers do rather hazard and endamage a matter than help it: these and many others are to be considered in the ordaining of magistrates.

But this again and again I deem worthy to be spoken, that very well it is and most meet that the administration of the common weale should be committed unto old men, which both by reason of their age and experience in matters have most skill: for true is that sentence of Plato, and which of Cicero is holden as it were for an oracle,

> Blessed may that man be counted, to whom even in his old age it
> hath chanced to obtain both wisdom and true opinions.

Crantor, an ordinary scholar of Xenocrates and most excellent philosopher, reckoning the state of man's life and deciphering by most wise division our actions and cogitations, affirmed that the first part of our life is to be employed unto virtue: the second to good health: the third to honest pleasure: and the fourth as he thought unto riches. For doubtless, nothing that good or pleasant is can happen unto us without virtue: next unto this (as the best companion of virtue) he deemed to be good health. For scarcely can it be will with us in our mind when it is evil with our body, and scarcely can the grief of the body be without the grief of the mind. Moreover, he that is in good health enjoyeth freer mind and is not frustrated of the quietness of his wit and senses: next unto these two, let honest pleasure come as a third companion, which then doubtless is chief and best, when the mind enjoyeth itself: it measureth all things unto the tranquility and pleasures of the mind: it is not delighted with the tickling of the senses or allurements of the body, but in contemplation of great and weighty matters, which surely be the food of an honest mind well furnished with liberal studies. That fourth part which hath society with the former three, although it be the least of all, yet when we respect human necessity and when we consider that man hath need of meat, drink, apparel, and dwelling house, it cannot be accounted otherwise than necessary. For as Callymachus saith, without riches, virtue advanceth no man: and that virtue without riches doth little or nothing adorn any man. Theognis the true poet testifieth that for fear of poverty we go headlong even into the seas: for penury now and then urgeth excellent persons and compelleth them to attempt very hard enterprises. Plantus, the most pleasant among the comical poets, for want and scarcity of victuals, placed himself for hire to grind in a mill, and there so often as he had any vacant time from his work, he accustomed himself to write comedies and to sell them.

Cassius Severus, also an excellent orator, having continued for the space of 15 years a vanished man, died in great penury, scarcely having rags wherewith to cover his privities. And Valerius, the companion in office of Brutus, died so poor that he was buried at the common costs of the city. And the legitimate son of king Perseus (as Marcellinus writeth) after his miserably calamity and frowning fortune, was glad to practice the smith's occupation to get his living withal: these cogitations ought oftentimes to be involved in mind of all them that will rightly constitute human society.

They that take upon them the office of a magistrate: let them know that they bear a majesty of the common weale, and let them forget themselves so long to be private persons, as they execute or use the administration of a public office: let the magistrates evermore have before their eyes, the laws of the common weale, whereunto in all points let them know that obedience is to be given. For as the laws do govern the magistrates, so the magistrates ought to govern the people. For true is that proverb to be pronounced by Tully:

> *The magistrate is law, that doth speak and dispute:*
> *But the law is a magistrate silent and mute.*

For this happeneth in a good common weale, that he which modestly obeyeth may seem worthy and meet sometime to bear authority: and it is expedient that he which obeyeth the laws should hope to bear rule in time to come: and he that is in office and hath jurisdiction or governance, let him think that not long after it may come to pass that he must obey others: let the first retain virtues as to their guides to direct and rule them, without the which nothing is well done, whereof the first and principal is justice, which layeth the foundation of human society and containeth in it godliness: which Sextus Empiricus teacheth to be the knowledge of worshiping God aright. For this virtue especially respecteth the divine reverence, mysteries, and ceremonies: without the which nothing orderly, neither anything holily or godly can be done in a common weale.

It is the nature of justice to hurt no man, nor to injure any: to give to every man that which is his right: to reward those that deserve well, with favor, praise, and gifts, and those that deserve evil, with losses, reproach, shame, punishments, and death: but moreover, a right excellent duty of justice is in word and deed to keep faith and promise: for nothing can be more filthy in those which bear sway in the public weal than to break promise, which reproach doubtless is never blotted out with oblivion, as we read of the Carthaginians, whom Ennius the poet called faithless, or league-breakers, because they started from their leagues and promises: which was the only and chiefest cause why that city which (for the empire of the whole world) contended so many years with the people of Rome, (the chief vanquishers of all other nations) was destroyed.

Prudence, the second virtue, consisteth in choice or discerning of good and bad, and is the ringleader or chief of other virtues: insomuch that Apollophanes, a worthy philosopher, said: that this only was the virtue upon whom all the rest were attendant. Temperance (notwithstanding) helpeth very much, and so shineth in all our doings, that she is thought to be the moderatrix or directeress thereof: this is she which with so long continued praise hath extolled that worthy sentence of Solon, warning us to do: *nothing too much.*

The children of the Persians were carefully taught and trained to learn temperance, which to the end that they should the more diligently observe—their rulers appointed and commanded certain of the discreetest old men in their cities—to be present at their daily exercises: to the end that, they fearing the looks and grave countenances of their ancient overseers, might in all their doings be governed and directed by modesty and temperance, to frame themselves thereafter in all things, from time to time, accordingly. Constancy must also be there linked and annexed, namely that which is of words and deeds counted the most faithful observer or keeper: she causeth that the secrets of the public weal be kept close and in silence, than the which there can be no better thing: for which virtue the Persians especially are praised, which doe use to keep all their secrets most faithfully: neither fear, neither hope, nor any other fair promise can allure them to utter any secret matter that is to be concealed: for they have an old lesson or rule among them, whereby they are advertised: that silence is kept with danger of life. Neither are they thought able to achieve any great exploit, which are not able to bridle their tongues, which member nature hath ordained as the easiest of all others: thereby to show that silence is no hard virtue to be kept and observed.

Aristotle saith that there be three things necessary in a magistrate: first, that he embrace justice and the other virtues, thereby to direct all those things which are profitable for the common weale. Next, that he do love the present state of his city, and being therewith content, enterprise to do nothing either newfangled or strange, but to go that way which their ancestors have instituted: and which, by the treading steps of others, was worn plain: for desire of new alterations and things is rather wont to weary and weaken the common weale than to make the same better by any means. Thirdly, that magistrates should have power of the people, sufficient to execute those things which appertain to their function or office: which thing doubtless causeth that they themselves, with greater courage bear out their office: and those again shall more diligently obey them, unto whom obeisance is to be given.

All magistrates which have the deciding of laws and which do exercise any kind of revenge or punishment against offenders, ought as some bold opinion to be strangers: for as they themselves say: private grudges, enmities, and hatred do arise amongst citizens, when as one citizen punisheth another: but on the other part, fellow citizens are more tractable and prone to show favor one towards other than as if the matter were in the dealing of a stranger: by the reason whereof, many people of the Italians have accustomed to send for such magistrates from other places: but to be short, I am of opinion that in a well governed common weale, wherein all men be obedient to the laws and customs of their country, citizen magistrates are far better and govern much more honorably than strangers: which thing doubtless, not only by the Romans, Carthaginians, Athenians, and Lacedaemonians, but by diverse others, which commit all offices unto their citizens, may be perceived: but especially it is evident by the noble common weale of the Venetians, wherein there is no place given to strangers: and yet, notwithstanding, there is neither severity wanting, nor by such manner of judgments any discords do arise, neither any seditions or enmities grow.

And one thing concerning that common weale of the Venetians, we may well say, which I cannot remember that every I read or saw elsewhere: for the order of that city never swerved or altered from the order and state wherein by the first founders thereof it was constituted and ordained: but hath always remained in one state of government immutable: for they that builded that city devised amongst themselves and their magistrates, a reward (as it were) for their travails: and this inheritance left they unto their posterity, that no alien or denizen, born in any other country, should be admitted to bear any office or authority amongst them: and so since that time, perpetually hath this order been observed, almost a thousand years, until this day: wherefore the posterity of them that first builded the city have always been rulers in the same city, and were called senators, seniors, fathers, and nobles, and all the rest commoners.

The chief and principal care for the common weale consisteth in senators, which ought to have authority, as well in times of wars as in time of peace: unto whom also from the other magistrates, men may appeal: these senators also (according to the institution of Lycurgus) are the keepers and reformers of the laws, and often as need shall require do constitute new [laws], by certain learned lawyers of their seignory: for it is a very hard thing to compass and comprehend all things in writ laws: for new affairs oftentimes happen and occur through the disorder of men, for redress whereof new laws are expedient, and all things daily prove, worse and worse, which by the laws are to be punished.

Solon the philosopher decreed no law against Parricides and murderers: being demanded why he had omitted the same, he answered, that he never thought that any such mischievous and wicked act could be committed or done by any man.

All order of the public weal, and all counsel, ought in doubtful cases and adverse affairs to come from the senators and counselors who be called fathers of their country, because even as parents provide of duty for their children, so ought the senators for their citizens and countrymen. Let these grave counselors, as it were, grow together into one body, which seeth with many eyes, worketh with many hands, and standeth upon many feet, which things surely bringeth to pass that the common weale is far better governed than the state of one Prince, for he alone forecasteth and foreseeth what he can: yet cannot he measure and compass all things by counsel and reason: for no one mortal man hath the knowledge of all things. And he is counted and reputed for the wisest who is ignorant in fewest matters: for many learned, wise, and grave men, laying their heads and devises together, do foresee all things; nothing is to them obscure; nothing happeneth suddenly and unlooked for; nothing new, nothing strange, nothing great or wonderful.

There if the senators themselves do trespass, they seem to offend more by their example than by the crime itself: for all the inferiors do follow their steps and think themselves scarcely to transgress, where as they see any senator guilty of the same crime. Let them therefore be firm and constant, not vain and lying, neither given to filthy lucre: let them not only banish away all filthy usury, but also all gain wherein may be any suspicion of filthiness.

Publius Scipio Nasica, unto whom the surname of a good man was by the senate bestowed, who did so many notable exploits for his country, on a certain time standing in election for the office of Aedileshippe, took a certain country fellow by his hard and rough hand, and, feeling the same so hard, demanded of him in sport whether he used to walk upon his feet or upon his hands: which thing was so grievously taken of the country fellow and other bystanders, that it came to the knowledge of the common people and was the cause why this excellent senator Scipio had a repulse in his suit: forasmuch as all the country people thought themselves to be hand in derision and made flouting stocks.

Very little or nothing do laws and institutions profit except they be grounded upon sacred scriptures, the author whereof is Almighty God himself: for if those ancient people which knew not God, but were led with certain superstitions and false religion, did nothing appertaining to the common weale without authority of their high bishops: what behooveth us Christians to do, which only embrace the true religion and which have Christ the Son of God for the founder and author of our religion? Surely we ought to endeavor with all care and diligence, that nothing be done, nothing thought upon or devised, except God his assistance and goodwill be thereto favorable, and that all our purposes, mysteries, or devises tend to his honor and glory, by whom we attain life everlasting: therefore, God's divine operations ought to go before the ordinances of man: according to this saying, *Imprimis venerare Deos*, first above all things worship God. The senator's charge and duties therefore shall be diligently to watch and care that no laws be established and enacted, but such as be consonant and agreeable to God's good pleasure: for if he be aiding and well pleased with our Christian rites and ordinances, there can nothing go amiss in the common weale, neither can there any sinister thing or mishap chance therein.

At the beginning, the governance of human affairs was in the authority of the bishops: and kings being initiated in sacred lore, took charge, both of divine and human things, neither thought they that any man could possibly rule well which was ignorant in sacred matters and estranged from God: therefore, in those days, either the priests themselves did govern, or else the princes did attempt nothing without their advice and authority. For Romulus, at the first foundation and beginning of Rome, called the bishop which had charge in the temples and holy ceremonies by the names of kings and reigning, as it were, with a mutual or associate authority, would have him to be the keeper of the laws and traditions of their country: and not without cause, for the Prelates being inspired with the Holy Ghost do teach and instruct us throughly in the precepts of holiness and immortality.

There are two times to be considered upon: the one of peace, the other of wars: and as in time of wars, circumspect care for peace may not be omitted, so in time of peace such thing sought to be foreseen which in time of wars may serve and be most necessary: for surely it is a point of great wisdom to haste and have in readiness, in the time of peace, such things which fear of wars should compel us speedily to have in use and to occupy: both these considerations therefore must be carefully looked to, by them that bear chief rule and authority, that with warlike munitions that may defend and maintain the sweet joys of peace, and that the munitions of wars be not prejudicial or hindering to the maintenance of peace. For the Romaines, the most excellent of all others, unto the chiefest office appointed to Consuls: the one to deal in the affairs for the city's behoof, and the other in warlike matters: for [little] should it prevail them to live at rest and quietness within the walls of the city, if in the fields all were in hurlyburly and uproar, or if their enemies were not kept back from invading their territories: and on the other part, to hold wars abroad, and, at home to want advice or counsel, were very dangerous.

That promotions or offices should be perpetual in the common weale, I think it to be perilous: for the long continuance thereof doth often alter men's manners: and now and then giveth them occasion of tyrannous practices, as we may well see of Julius Caesar, who, being continual Dictator, invaded the public weal. For it is much harder in prosperity to observe modesty than in adversity; and therefore, that custom is to be commended and allowed whereby the two Consuls be appointed for no longer space than one year. The Consul ought diligently to be careful in mustering for the wars, that in every precinct the wealth, number, and age be regarded: for those soldiers obey unwillingly and are negligent in their duty, which are forced beyond their ability and power: and very ill fareth it with that army which thinks themselves, without just occasion, forced to warfare; and when this Consul hath mustered soldiers, let him not suffer them to harbor or lodge in the wintering places, under covert, but let them lodge abroad in the open field, yea, if it were in a peaceable time: and let him teach them, that soldiers are of no more force than their Captains and General: for all men affirm that this sentence of Homer is true:

> *More safe is an host of harts, a lion being guide:*
> *than a host of lions which an hart have on their side.*

Special consideration and care must be had for the due administering and execution of laws in a good common weale, which surely causeth that men do live without violence of injury: for it is impossible for a multitude to live without strife, especially in that city where all things be common: albeit we say it is much better for every man to have his own: for we see that fields which are in common amongst many lie untilled and grow full of brambles and briers: but private fields, far more neat and trimly husbanded: but private patrimonies be they which make men diligent and attendant, and measure herein is to be prescribed unto them, lest rich men enjoy all and the poorer and weaker sort [be] clean thrust out and defrauded.

Varro saith that variance at the beginning took his first name of contention for limits or bounds: which thing indeed Virgil seemeth to affirm where he saith:

Limes agro positus, litem ut discerneret aruis.

There was set and ordained a limit or bound,
To avoid contention in fallowed ground.

For now and then contention ariseth for debarring or stopping the course of rainwater or of other matters which daily happen in fields, or else in the cities, when men do argue and stand in contention for the walls of their houses: for droppings of their house eves and of rafters not fastened: and oftentimes it comes to pass that amongst merchants, contentions may arise, and specially when many are found vain and double-dealers, with whom a man must not deal in secret means, but before some arbitrators or secret witnesses and judges. Such manner of strifes whereby enmity and heart-burnings may grow ought to be straightway by composition to be determined and ended, that the citizens may be brought into concord, which then is brought to pass when every man enjoys his own, obtaineth his due right, and all variance or dissension set apart.

Upon holydays and such days as are appointed for either fairs or feasts, it shall be good to stay prosecution of causes and matters judicial, which thing also is customly frequented in any public joy or mourning.

A Praetor amongst the Romaines was so called because he bear rule: and he was called Urbanus amongst the citizens administered the laws. It was in the power of the Praetor to minister both public and private authority, therefore it is needful that the Praetors be men of upright dealing and well deserving of the public weal: who ought in no part to be ignorant of the laws and customs of the common state, but plainly and absolutely to be so skillful in laws both public and private, that nothing appear unto them either obscure or doubtful. Let good and conscionable lawyers plead causes and handle nothing with craft and malengine: but let them speak all things truly, and let them not leave a lie unpunished: for there ought to be nothing in a common weale so uncorrupt and sincere as judgment: which surely is more often corrupted with speech than with money: whereupon very well said Cicero, that he understood not why he that corrupteth judgment with money, should be worthy of punishment, [whereas] he that corrupts it with eloquence should have praise: to me (saith he) it rather appeareth that he offendeth more in this point which rather with speech than with money corrupteth the judge: because no man with money can corrupt a wise judge, but with smooth and dissembling speech any man may: for how are the corrupters of causes worthy to be hated, and how grievously are they to be punished? For they do sell the patronage of justice and forsake the best office in the world, which is defending right: sometime they pinch and get money from the defendant, sometime again poule the plaintiff, and in the end delude them both: and many do very ill, which take on them the patronage or office of defending the client, and do handle the same so coldly that they differ little from forgers of causes: for true is that sentence of Cicero which saith: perhaps men cannot be defended without dispraise, and that negligently to be defended could not be without great wickedness.

Let lawyers therefore and patrons of causes plead their clients' causes, and that for duty's sake, that they may deserve well of the citizens; and let their reward be to have a good report in all men's mouths, and let it not be lawful for them, if by any means it may, that they take any bribe or gift for handling the cause, as it was established by the law called Cincia: for a filthy thing it is and not worthy any man, to set out the tongue for gain or lucre in pleading causes. Surely Antipho Rhamnusius (as antiquity reporteth) was the first that ever for defense of any cause took reward, whose example long times after, the Grecians and Latins followed: saying that the merchandise of the tongue was of far other sort than any other merchandise whatsoever: but the Romans, from whom all good examples as well of honesty as of virtue are to be taken, by the law of Cincia prescribed an order unto the covetousness of orators and pleaders of causes; and because young men puffed up with the hope of gain should not be permitted negligently to handle matters, at the request of Appius Claudius, they suffered the law Cincia to be moderated.

Unto those magistrates which we authorize to have the administering of justice, we rather ought to impart some stading fee or public stipend, than private gain: lest thereby the judgments of the law be set to port sale, which thing no doubt is prejudicial unto all people: and for the most part, the common decay of the public weal: whether the judgment be corrupted or whether else anything be done by deceit or violence by them which be judges and have jurisdiction in executing justice.

Overseers of shamefastness and modesty are so necessary in a common weale, that without them, little or nothing do other magistrates prevail: for there cannot be a more commodious thing than to have people well mannered with civility: wherefore the gravest persons and most approved in virtue (some out of every several tribe or ward) are hereunto to be admitted: which may reform and redress the manners of the city, lest thereby there creep in peevish customs, pernicious both toe the people and to the whole city: therefore, great diligence is to be required, that the manners of the people be most sincere and perfect: and then again, that no pernicious custom do invade the citizens, than the which there can nothing in cities happen worse: and lastly, that the religion and ceremonial orders which have been by our elders well established be also well observed.

The Romans called the censure of shamefastness and modesty, the Lady and Mistress of discipline: and them which bore offices in the common weale, they called Censors, which took their name of judging, controlling, constituting, and commanding: of what effect it is very well to discharge and execute this office, even hereby may we perceive in that this office of dignity of Censor did give the surname unto Cato Censorius, who very ell executed this same function. The infamy which we call the Censors check, was far more grievously taken of the Romans than any other punishment, and sometimes the rigor thereof stretched against the magistrates: for the senators were case out of the senate house by the Censors check, as we read of Lucius Antonius, because he put away from him a young virgin whom he had married: none of his friends being called to counsel: so we read also of Lucius Flaminius, who caused certain to be put to death, for looking lasciviously at certain women whom they loved: also Caius Fabricius the Censor, removed out of the senate house Public Cornelius, a noble personage, because he brought ten pounds worth of plate to a certain banquet. Fat and corpulent soldiers, perfumed with ointment, were noted with this check, their hoses taken from them, and they dismissed and discharged out of the host.

In judgments of life and death, great care and heed ought to be had: for civil hatreds and private conspiracies then burst forth unto revenge, when as the magistrates have power of life and death: and therefore the Romaines, when they had appointed their Consuls unto whom they committed the special charge of the common weale: yet was it not lawful for them to execute or put to death any citizen of Rome, and truly not without good cause: for nothing more procureth the destruction of the weal public than the punishment by death of those which specially have but little dealt with others, or whose crimes or offenses have not so far come to light as by no means they can or may be denied, or else that they be apparently known unto all men: for that worketh a perpetual injury, when suspicion of innocency remaineth in the peoples' heads, of them which through false or rash judgment are said to be unjustly condemned, for innocency carrieth with it great favor, and the rumor or muttering of the people striketh fear into them which have condemned innocents. And moreover, the fore of conscience brings to pass that such persons as have so overreached themselves are thought never to live in security, but appoint unto themselves present punishment before their eyes. How notable is that sentence of Julius Caesar, which with often repetitions he would use,

> A wretched companion of old age truly,
> Is the memory of ancient cruelty.

And therefore, they that must give sentence and judgment of the life and spirit of man, which is part of the world and hath a mind by the special gift of God, partaking of reason, and filling up the number of the living, ought carefully to advise and consult with deliberation and not to do anything with rash judgment, because such a deed once done cannot be called back again.

Alexander, king of Macedonie, unto his mother Olympias, urging him greatly to kill a certain guileless person, requesting the king's consent thereto, in consideration of that nine month's space which she bore him in her womb: most gently thus answered, "O good mother, rather request or demand any other reward at my hands: for man's life cannot be acquitted or recompensed with any good turn or benefit."

Sabacus, moreover, king of the Egyptians (a man for godliness and religion famous), as Diodorus Siculus maketh mention, did so much abhor shedding of blood that he commanded convicted and condemned persons, being bound with chains, to become slaves for the city, rather than that they should be put to death: doubtless true is that tragical sentence, and in heart and mind, evermore to be recited and recorded of them which do bear rule, viz.,

> *Whatever thou be that does rule or reign:*
> *From shedding blood, leave and abstain.*

There was wont to be amongst the Romaines eight kinds of punishments, that is to say: amercements, banishment, imprisonment, whipping, recompense of as much for trespass made, reproach, bondage, and death: yet seldom with death did the Romans accustom to pursue, except against Parrycides, murderers, rebels, and such like wicked persons, whose lives were not to be spared. But now an ill custom hath taken place, that thieves even for small matters are executed by death and so they take away that which can never be restored unto mortal men. The great consideration for the common treasure in a common weale ought to be had: for treasures and money are counted the sinews or strengths of the city, without the which it can scarcely be preserved: for these things do beautify a city in prosperity, and bring ready succor in adversity: wherefore there are to be ordained treasurers which may have the authority of receiving, keeping, and laying out of the common treasure: these men ought to be grave and upright, and ought to abstain their hands from public and private corruption: not unhonest troublesome persons, but which can diligently measure the rate of fortune and of such persons as they shall have to deal withal, and besides this let them take heed that publicans and tollers extort nothing by violence or crafty collusion from them over whom they have rule: for that kind of people is odious, and now and then, by reason of their unhonest dealing and lewd demeanor, provoketh and stirreth the common people to desire of newfangleness.

In living of tributes and taxations, treasurers ought to be gentle and seldom times to do it: for it grieveth the citizens to have their proper and private stock and substance employed on public affairs: except in great distress or time of danger, for then all good citizens do of their own good accord fall in consideration hereof, and willing be contributory to payment: but if they may spare their private substance, they live better contented: and if there be no other remedy, but to do otherwise, then ought they to entreat all men gently, thereby the more easily to raise their tributes and win the people's hearts withal: for far more is the goodwill of citizens to be esteemed than any mass of substance of treasures. Noble was the saying of Alexander the Great, when on a time being demanded where he had his treasures laid up, answered: he had laid them up with his friends and well-willers, and that they were well and warily kept to his use there: for goodwill and good love is the lady, both of a man's own substance and of another man's also. Tiberius Caesar, also unto his Lieutenants, receivers, or treasurers which counseled him to exact tribute of his provinces and countries, answered, that it was the part of a good shepherd to shear his sheep and not to fleece them.

They that be authorized to coin money ought to obey the commandment of the treasurer, lest they forge or abase the coin, or mingle it with any other base metal, for it is most dangerous to make counterfeit money of less value than it should be: the consideration whereof is most diligently to be overseen of the treasurers: some do suppose that the word *Moneta* is called so properly because it giveth warning that no deceit in money, stamp, or weight be made or used; but the name of Pecunia, as Varro saith, took his beginning of Pecus: for the riches and substance of men in times past consisted in Pecoribus: that is to say, in cattle. And this thing doth Lucius Columella testify to be true, and Ovid (libro 5). Fastoru maketh mention where he saith:

> *All other instruments as yet were not fore use out found.*
> *The wealthy, cattle did possess, or else great store of ground.*
> *And hereupon were richmen called, hereof hath money name.*
> *But now unlawfully each man, to seek for wealth doth frame.*

Cambyses, the father of Cyrus, king of Persia, being asked by what means cities might be kept in the best safeguard, answered: if they which keep the same cities do think they can never be wary enough of their enemy. The saying of this most wise king is always to be revolved of them which bear authority in a common weale: for what availeth armor? What munitions? What are the walls and towers profiting unto them which negligently keep and look to their watches and wards? For we see very many cities by negligence of their watches and scouts (with the sudden coming of their enemies) put to the spoil and sacked: and moreover, as touching night watches, to whom citizens trusting and sleeping soundly, have not known anything of the coming of their enemy, until the scaling ladders have been set up to their walls and they thrown down headlong from the tops of their turrets.

Spargapyses, the son of Tomyris, queen of Scythia, being together with all his host of men drunk with wine and slumbering or sleepy, were in that estate altogether destroyed: and doubtless, no scouts, nor watches can more safely or diligently be exercised than of them which bear the chiefest authority, whether the same be in the tents or within the walls, certain it is scarce safe enough for the citizens to sleep soundly when they shall perceive the chief overseers of the watchmen to be wanting: and a captain seemeth to commit his host to the hazard of fortune, so long as he sleepeth.

Alexander of Macedonie hath left us a good lesson for this matter, who, because he would not be deceived by means of sleep, used as he lay in his bed to stretch out his arm (having under the same a brasen bowl or basin standing) and to hold in his hand a ball of silver, to the intent that when sleep had wearied and taken away the force of his fingers, hearing the fall of the silver ball into the bowl or basin, he should straightway by the noise and sound thereof awake again out of sleep. Surely this lesson I think that most excellent king learned of the cranes, which do use a nightly watch among themselves always, and because they would not be deceived or betrayed by any mishap in their sleep, they stand upon one leg holding a little stone in the other, which when it falleth from them by hitting the other standing leg, or making a noise with lighting on the ground, they are thereby awakened out of their sleep.

Even so with no less care ought they to watch which bear authority in a common weale, that in such manner they may set in order their watches and keep the holds of their city, that the common weale sustain no discommodity nor dishonor thereby, neither in time of wars, neither yet in time of peace. Doubtless Socrates in Plator used great diligence and care, in the choice of such as should keep watch and ward: and surely the better and more well their citizens be, the more fit persons are they to keep watch and ward: which otherwise we see falleth out in rude or barbarous cities, wherein laborers, workmen, porters, and poor men are put to scouts and watch: but the richer men cocker themselves and live at ease within their own houses. Sometimes watches are committed in charge unto the soldiers only, which now and then being wearied with their daily travail, either watch recklessly or else sleep so soundly, that they are not to be awakened with any noise at all: as it chanced unto those Romans which kept their capitol when it was besieged by the Frenchmen: which Romaines had not they been awakened out of their sleep by the gaggling of a goose, had been utterly undone, and the common weale of the Latins forever extinguished.

Let there be placed orderly upon the walls in places fir for that purpose, two warders which must have given them a watchword, lest they be deceived: and let them be called upon and punished which sleep in their watchtime. Let the scouts in the daytime watch before the gates, on the towers, at loopholes, or at other chosen places, lest that a multitude of guests unlooked for come, as it were, between them and home, and take away booties, carry away captives, and invade the city: with no less care also let the night watches be placed in the city than upon the walls: for most mischievous deeds are rather put in practice by night than by day. Thieves, harlots, cutthroats, and robbers are no less to be restrained than public enemies, against whom doubtless needful it is that the overseers of the watch should extend punishment with great severity, if they will rightly provide for the good estate of their city: for worst of all fareth it with that city wherein harlots and night-thieves, ravaging in the same, be not sufficiently met withal.

It was lawful among the Romaines by the law of twelve tables to kill a night thief: so hath it also been lawful to do to an adulterer taken with the manner, and also to a woman committing fornication. These notwithstanding I judge are not to be permitted, but in such manner to be handled, that for fear of punishment all men keep themselves at home from doing evil abroad: for he loveth to do nothing that is good or right which shunneth daylight, and he that stealeth in lurking manner is afraid lest some should see him and bewray him, and so thinketh the night more safe for him than the day time.

It was not wont only to be the charge of them that had the oversight of the watches amongst the Romaines to exercise watches and wars upon the walls, but also it was enjoined that they should be vigilant against all night travelers: whereby the public quietness of the city might be preserved and maintained: moreover these and such like watches do help in many other matters, and especially in avoiding casualties of fire, which surely are seen to be most dangerous in cities: for both do they quench casual chances of fire within the city happening, and also oftentimes do catch in a trip subtle fires of houses, whose offense therein is to be accounted capital and worthy of death: and them also which negligently rake up their fires, they ought to punish by whipping and cudgeling.

Dinocrates, an excellent architect of Macedonie, having promised unto Alexander the Great to raise up the hill called Athon in Thracia, of a monstrous height unto the similitude and resemblance of a man, whose left hand should support the walls of a most large city and the right hand should hold a bowl, which should receive the floods descending from the hill and pour them into the sea: Alexander (being delighted with the devise of this figure) asked him whether there were any fields near unto it to nourish and maintain the city with corn and victual, yea or no?

Dinocrates answered: that it must have succor and relief from beyond the seas: the king said that such a devise was not to be allowed at all, for (saith he) as the infant lately born into the world can neither live nor prosper without the milk of the nurse, so neither can a city be sustained or cherished without the fruits of the fields.

The example of this noble king, Alexander, ought to exhort all builders of cities to appoint the situation thereof in plentiful and fruitful places, and that they which have charge over the people do especially provide corn and victuals for their sustenation: for little should the defense and safeguard of the city prevail to small purpose, should the laws, rites {rights?}, and order of a city serve, if the people should starve for hunger: for what can be more dangerous among that people, whom neither armor, magistrates, neither God's justice, nor man's laws, neither any shame can keep in straight order than dearth and famine: for very aptly hereunto saith Lucanus the poet, *Nescit plebs ieuna timere.*

Let therefore first and principal care be for competent provision of victual, namely bread corn, the use whereof is seen to be far more necessary than any other thing, and let there be made purveyors or principal victuallers, to have the oversight and survey of all victual, and make provision of the same accordingly: let the corn be kept for common use, either in deep trenches, clean fanned from the chaff and covered over, whereby for seven years store it may be well reserved, or in broad grainers, with little windows, on the north end thereof, wherein for three years space it may be preserved from the moth, weevil, and all noisome vermin: and let them have a special care that there be no corn or grain carried forth of the city, but in great store and plenty thereof, lest it become musty: but let it rather be brought in by exchange and rechange made from the countries near adjoining, for it were far better to have store enough at home sufficiently, not only to serve them and their country but also, if need were, to help our distressed neighbors. And let them set a rate or price of things, lest they being bestowed at the will of them that shall sell them, they be rated and esteemed as it shall seem good unto them at all times.

Regard also must be had that not with a little care and diligence the temples and churches of the immortal God (which with such great costs and charges are edified, and which make the cities specially thereby far more gorgeous) have such officers and overseers for the government thereof, lest otherwise by negligence and sloth they fall to ruin or decay: wherefore Aediles are to be appointed, which thereupon were called by the Romaines, by that name Aediles, because (as Varro saith) they had the oversight of sacred and private houses. It was also the charge of the same officers, amongst the Romaines, to see that the common streets and highways should be well leveled and made even, and that the same should be kept in decent order, and that thereupon no building should be erected and set which either might hinder the commodity or comeliness of the same: also they had a charge enjoined them, to see that the water conduits, common sewers, and skins should be cleansed and scoured, and that the bridges should be repaired and amended: moreover, there is nothing in a free city which doth more breed envy or hatred than to see certain fellow citizens in a short time enriched with the common money or treasure, whereas the same could not suffice them all.

Book 4

ADRIANUS CAESAR was a Prince of excellent wit and exquisite learning: for oftentimes he both wrote, spake, heard others speak, and talked with his friends at once, and would do all this at one time: he was also greatly given to poety and a favorer of all good sciences: in arithmetic, geometry, music, and painting most skillfill: he often was wont to say that the common weale is so to be regarded of them which bear rule in the same, that everyone should know how that he had to do for the common weale and not for his own proper and private estate.

Phocion the Athenian (when as abundance of treasures was sent unto him of gift from Philip king of Macedonia) would not take any of it at all: and to the king's ambassadors exhorting him that if he himself could easily lack the same treasures, yet at the least to take it for his children's use: for whom (said they) it was very hard being in such penury and distress as they were, to maintain their father's dignity: he answered, if my children do resemble and be like to me their father in condition, this little plot of ground which hath brought and maintained me to this dignity, shall also suffice to bring up and maintain them: but if they do not resemble me, sure I will not maintain their riot with these treasures and riches.

In no place at these days is found that land which of its own fruitfulness nourisheth the cyclops without tillage and sowing: neither is that Erithrea of Lusitania which men say Gerion sometimes possessed, being so rank and fruitful soil that when once the corn is cast upon the ground, the new sprouting seed soon bringeth forth new blades and beareth seven or rather more harvests one after another: neither floweth in our coasts that flood Nylus, which of itself bringeth forth an herb called Lotos, whereof men in those parts do make bread to eat, and whereof with such greatness (as Homer saith) they do eat, that they altogether forget the ordering of their household affairs: wherefore men must provide to have possession of lands, that provision of victuals may be reserved from time to time.

Marcus Curius hath by his wisdom taught us to have great store of public lands: and that private men should have so much thereof, as to the maintaining of their life and living, should be necessary: for when as he out of his triumphs had adjudged innumerable acres of land to the common weale, to every man in several he only allotted forty, neither reserved he any greater portion thereof unto himself than the rest had. He was blamed of certain persons because he had given himself the least part and had entitled the common weale to the most part: he said unto them, that no man ought to think that ground to be a little or insufficient which should suffice his own use and his family's.

As it behooveth civil society to have few to bear authority and many to obey, so in household affairs there ought to be one which should have chief rule, and he be ancient in years, and all the residue to obey. And as in a city by due obedience to laws, the magistrate is said to govern others justly, so in commanding and obeying, we have accustomed to govern domestical dealings. Let them which bear authority or office in a common weale know that the laws do govern and are above them, and let them that are the chief of an household follow the rule of a good husband or householder. There is therefore a good order in some cities, that none may be chosen into the senate which hath not the charge of house and family.

He that is the governor of a household ought always to remember that he hath sometimes been a servant, that he do rather correct offenses with words than with stripes, and had rather that his family should fear his severity and justice than tremble at his cruelty: for it goeth worst of all with that family which rather with fear than with zeal goeth about their business. And furthermore in great travails and in executing weighty offices or duties, it behooveth the householder to show himself the first man, officious, and diligent: for the inferiors will be ashamed of sloth and sluggishness when they shall see the elder to be diligent and painful: so on the other part, he shall beware and take heed that he do nothing filthily which his household may have in suspicion: for they do far more offend by example which bear authority than in committing offense.

Amongst the ancient in times past there was such multitude of slaves that they by violence thrust the freemen out of certain cities, and now and then rebelliously received and withstood their masters coming homewards by force of arms: for we read that the people of the country of Scythia were a nation almost invincible, for they did not only withstand Darius king of Persia from enterprising upon their costs and borders, but also put him to a vile and shameful flight: moreover they overthrew the hosts of

Alexander, they established the Empire of the Parthians, and people of Bactrians, they had Asia tributary unto them 1500 years, from which country, when as these Scythians returned with conquest in their third expedition (for they had been 8 years absent from their wives) they were at the first driven back and forcibly repulsed from coming home by their own servants and bondmen. For their wives, wearied with longlooking for their husbands, new-married themselves to their bondslaves which were left at home to keep their cattle: which slaves not without slaughter and bloodshed withstood and would not suffer their masters at their return to come home into their own countries and houses. And although in the end the victory fell to their masters, yet notwithstanding they bickered and skirmished together so doubtfully, that hard it was to discern who in the end would get the upper hand: but at the last the bondmen, being utterly vanquished, were hanged upon gibbets, and the women stricken with remorse of their guilty and filthy consciences, dispatched and murdered themselves, partly by the halter and partly with the sword. Amongst the notorious wars of the Romaines, is not also the servile wars recounted and reckoned, which took the name of bondmen vanquished?

But sometimes slaves have shown forth examples of most tried faith and trustiness, as Caius Plotius Plancus witnesseth, for he being by the Triumuiri proscript and appointed to have been executed, for fear hid himself privily in a farm near Salern, when the soldiers that were sent to search him out, having by the savor of his perfumes smelled him out, caught his servants, who, being much and long time evil entreated and tormented [by the soldiers], would not disclose their master. Plancus, pitying and having compassion on the fidelity of his own servants, came forth amongst the midst of them and offered his throat into the hands of the soldiers, thereby to deliver his servants from present torments.

Marcus Antonius, also an excellent orator, being accused of incest, had experience in the fidelity of his servant, who being brought unto judgment, even he which bore the lantern to that ungracious act, being also tormented, scourged, racked with burning plates, scorched and half burned to death, would never declare his master's incest, whereunto he was privy and of counsel. So have there been also others in like manner approved: but the trustiness of servants to their master's is not always to be assayed.

The freeman which hath under him the government of servants ought specially to think that they are men and not brute beasts, and that he should not rage with cruelty against them in scourging, evil entreating, or chaining of them (for by scourging their hearts are made obdurate and hardened) neither do they anything but with evil will: but the master ought to deal more gently with them, exacting their daily tasks and that not without mercy: their diligence and good endeavor is to be commended, whereby they may apply themselves with cheerfulness in their labors and business. They ought also to have such food and sustenance given them which may strengthen their bodies without curiosity and costliness. Let their apparel be such as may cover their bodies decently in summer, and defend them from cold and rain in winter: for servants pinched with cold, over-awed with fear, and hunger-starved cannot perform any manner of office or duty of service.

We must also take heed, lest through straight looking to our servants they become desperate: for now and then they are given to be cruel against those that be weaker than themselves: and the blows or stripes of the master are sometimes revenged upon their children and wives.

We have yet fresh in our memory a servant of a wicked wit and cruel meaning: this fellow had a very rigorous master that often cudgeled and beat him cruelly, where at this his servant, being angry and not knowing how to be revenged upon his master, on a time caught two infants (which were his said master's children), the one of a year's age, the other of two year's, and with them, ascending up into a certain high turret, called his master and willed him to take his younger babes up into his lap: whom so soon as he had squatted to the ground he cast himself headlong after them, because he would not come alive into the danger of his master again.

Bondmen enthralled and endangered unto us by the law, by reason they are to us indebted, are more gently to be entreated till they have paid their duty: for we ought to remember that so soon as they have recompensed their debt with their bodily travail, that they are free born and not of servile condition, as are those franchised bondmen (who although freed) yet after freedom do owe some service unto use: wherefore we must account them as journeymen or laborers hired, and we must in all things use them as freemen with courtesy, we must require their work and allow reasonable wages, and truly pay the same to them: for to have their good report it shall much profit whensoever we shall be driven to hire other laborers.

Of all societies or fellowships, there is none more agreeable unto nature than the society of man and woman: for there is engraffed by nature in every living creature a love and zeal to their like of kind, and a reason of conservation by conjunction of male and female: for there can be no wild beast so cruel, so solitary, and alone wandering, which in their time do not seek a mate of their own kind and condition for procreation's sake: seeing then there is no such society or fellowship more according to nature than that of the male and female, it behooveth us to write of matrimonial conjunction especially when as a citizens do match themselves with citizens in marriage by a long continued goodwill, and so reconcile and make atonement between grudging enemies—as we read of Julius Caesar and Pompeius, whose affinity so long as it flourished did subdue and repress civil discord and reduced all the civil wars unto unity and concord.

For had not the ravished virgins of Sabina appeased the minds of their parents and husbands by the law of matrimony, the common weale of the Romaines had been utterly destroyed: very necessary therefore is it to entreat of marriage and natural amity: for man doth not only marry and take a wife for procreation's sake, but also to have a companion of life, with whom he may live together and participate either fortune, both prosperity and adversity: for he that is led by reason doth seek for the commodities of his life, neither seeth he that he can sufficiently provide for his own estate, except he take a wife: therefore man, when he hath provided him of a dwelling house, taketh a wife, that he may procreate children, to the end to live more commodiously and the better bear the chances of either fortune.

It is especially necessary for a man to seek a trade whereby to live, that he may be the better provided for in his old age and sickness: wherefore it is either requisite for him to exercise husbandry, or seafaring, or some other kind of honest trade, thereby to get convenient stay whereof to live.

Therefore our careful mother, dame nature, parent of humankind, hath ordained wedlock, to the end that not only the most pleasant but also the most profitable society of life might thereby be put in ure: therefore as Xenophon hath left in writing in his book of household affairs, the divine providence of God made women to be more fearful creatures than men, because the same fear and awe in the woman should frame her the better to keep home and be diligent: for awe and fear help much to the diligence of keeping, and natural effeminacy or tenderness hath delivered unto them trades and faculties wherein they may be exercised, and find themselves occupied even within their own houses: furthermore, for as much meat, drink, and clothes must needs be had and cared for, not in every place openly or in wild woods, but at home under the roof of the house and in the inner parts of the same, it hath been necessary for men to be occupied abroad in company and assemblies of men, where they meeting together may devise means by labor and industry to get such things as being brought home should be laid up in store in some convenient place of the house: the charge of dispensation or bestowing whereof is more convenient for the woman than for the man.

Aristotle did very well assign the cares of all such matters are are to be done abroad unto men, and of things to be done at home unto women: and he thinketh it very uncomely and not fitting that women should deal in matters which are to be done abroad, as also for men to have the ordering and disposing of things within doors, for all helps and defenses of man's life are more easily procured and gotten by marriage than by singlehood.

We ought to restore that unto nature which we have borrowed, as to give unto others life which our parents have given unto us, by reason whereof we obtain that our children should restore that unto us in our extreme age and weakness, which they have received of us, when they were not able to help themselves: let them, I say, nourish and maintain us in our decrepitcy when we lean upon our staff and be weak and feeble: even as we brought up them in their tender age, when we sustained and embraced them in our arms, when they first learned to creep: and by these means, the interchange of nature is perpetually fulfilled, and that which it cannot do in the simple generality is conserved and kept in space and kind.

Furthermore, the discommodities happening in our old age (which surely are innumerable) and the manifold kinds of diseases which do vex and torment barren old age, and, as it were by conspiracies, fall upon old men at once: by what other reason may they be suffered or by what comfort else may they be mitigated or assuaged, but by the hope and help which we have or ought to have in our children: for far less grievous do those evils seem, which happen unto the father stricken into extreme age, when he himself declining toward decay seeth his son's grow lusty of body, and every day more strong, than those things which unto a man without children do happen, which seeth and perceiveth the powers both of his body and mind to decay, and therewithal at once all hope of help and posterity to come to an end: but death itself (which unto all men is most grievous) doth bring somewhat the less grief unto them: who knowing themselves to be mortal persons and that they can live no longer than human condition or state will suffer them, do behold their children by them begotten, resembling them, to be called by their proper names, whereby they are as it were reserved still alive in the fame and report of men, even after their decease. For they that depart this world, leaving behind them no children, do carry with them the ruin of their race and offspring, and deserve evil of the common weale, yea, of mankind also are they wrapped in perpetual oblivion, neither leave they any step or imitation of their life afterwards amongst men at any time.

Therefore I think best for a civil man to take unto him a wife, not only for necessity's sake, but also to the end they may live with more pleasure and profit, with whom a thankful, pleasant, and acceptable society of life must be framed, not to fulfill the lust of the flesh but to procreate and increase issue, thereby to replenish the civil common weale which indeed is the proper respect and duty of marriage.

Aelius Commodus Uerus, Emperor of Rome, is said to have answered his wife very notable, when as she seemed to be offended at the filthiness of his life, and complained of his foreign pleasures: suffer me, wife (saith he), by other women to exercise my lust and sensuality, for a wife is the name of dignity and not of pleasure.

Socrates the Philosopher, when he had long time and much suffered his first wife Xantippa to be both angry and churlish against him (to Alcibiades marveling that he could bear with such a shrewd and bitter woman, and not banish her out of his house) made this answer: that in suffering such a Vixen in her behavior at home, he enured himself the better to put up those injuries and reproaches which were done to him abroad by others: for Socrates had two wives at one time the better thereby to perform throughly the effect of patience.

Metellus Numidicus, the great and eloquent Orator, while he was Censor discoursing of the marriage of wives in his oration, spake these words: My Lords, if we could be without wives we should all easily lack and be without that molestation? but because Nature hath so ordained, that neither with them can we live commodiously, and without them we cannot live at all, I think it better rather to provide for a perpetual safety than for a short or momentary pleasure.

Which manifest confession of the care and molestation of wiving was misliked of many of the citizens of Rome, for the said that Metellus the Censor, whose purpose should have been to exhort the common people unto matrimony, could not confess or utter any thing touching the griefs and discommodities thereof, lest in so doing he should rather seem to dissuade the people from matrimony than exhort them thereunto: for so much as almost there is nothing throughout the whole life of man can be found which in every part of itself is absolute and perfect, that no stable amity could be found, nor more abundant in all duty and godliness, than in matrimony.

Tiberius Gracchus willingly and of his own accord saved and redeemed his wife's life with his own death, for he finding at home two snakes, in this sort destined that, unless he killed one of them, he and all his household should perish and die; if he let the male escape, it should then be his chance to escape alive: but if the female, then should his wife Cornelia escape alive. He so entirely loved his wife and so much esteemed matrimony, that he rather chose to die himself than to survive his wife.

The wives of Mynias have left us an example of admiration: for their husbands hang imprisoned by the Lacedemonians and judged to die for conspiring against the state, looked for present execution according to custom in the night season: but their wives, making a pretense or excuse to go speak unto their husbands and take their last leave, obtained license of the keepers to go unto them, where, changing their apparel and dissembling their sorrows with their heads covered, suffered their husbands to depart and gave themselves to the death, to the end that they might deliver and set at liberty their husbands.

Moreover the too much cherishing that Augustus used towards his daughters made them more wanton and lascivious, whereupon Julia, when a certain severe and grave friend of hers went about to persuade her to follow the example of her father's frugality, she scornfully answered: my father forgets that he is Caesar, but I remember that I am Caesar's daughter: she outraged so far in dissolute living that she prostituted her body to all men: and when as men that knew well her filthy life marveled how she brought forth children so like to Agrippa her husband, seeing she had to do with so many men: she answered that she could lawfully entertain and admit adulterers after that she was great with child by her husband: for seldom doth the woman keep shamefastness that hath once lost her chastity.

There are some women which take pleasure to talk of their filthy demeanor, and declare the blemish or disease of their mind and body with filthy speech, thereby to appear more pleasantly conceited unto the world: as Popilia the daughter of Marcus to a certain man which marveled what should be the cause: that all beasts do never admit the male to cover them, but at due seasons when they would be made great with young, and women at all times desire the society of man: she answered: because they are beasts.

But let the husband look to it, that he give no occasion of filthiness or offense unto his wife: and let her take heed that she do not speak any filthy thing at any time in the presence of her husband, wherein some men do much offend which allure their wives with uncleanliness of words and filthiness of speech unto lust and concupiscence, and do instruct them in fables, whereby they are made more ready to venerous dalliance, and inflamed with strange loves: and the men now and then speak those things which are able enough to inflame even those women that be otherwise very cold affected.

Furthermore, let the husband far more diligently abstain from having to do with any other strange person, if he desire to have a chaste wife: for no injury doth more diminish or sooner break the holy society of marriage than for the one party, I will not say, to be only taken in adultery, but also in any slender suspicion thereof.

The Persians therefore very well did grievously punish adultery, to the intent that the society of matrimony might be made the more firm and stable.

The continency of the husband for the most part keepeth his wife in chastity and maketh the man himself to be far more commendable. Laelius, the friend of Scipio, is counted the happier in this one respect: that in all his lifetime he had the company of one only woman, that is to say, his own wife, whom he had and no more: for there are very few wives so modest and so loving to their husbands that they can willingly and patiently suffer and bear with their husband's harlots.

I remember that I have read (not without marveling) of one women, even Tertia, wife of the former Aemilius mother to Cornelia, who was of such gentleness and patience , that when she knew her husband (being the conqueror of Africa) to be hotly enamored of her handmaid, a beautiful piece, and knew well that he used her too familiarly: she always dissembled the matter, lest otherwise she should accuse her husband (that most excellent Gentleman) of intemperancy, and that which is more: she was so far from revenge, than when Aemilius was dead she set her handmaid at liberty and freely placed her in marriage (to one that served her husband) with no small dowry.

Surely a man shall find very few women in all the memory of man of this nature, that can suffer or bear with their husband's strumpets: therefore that good reason or argument used by the lawyers is to be openly fixed in the houses of men: wherein is given us for precept:

> *What ever Law a man would have*
> *an other to observe:*
> *From that let not himself digress,*
> *nor once aside to serve.*

For what is more reproachful than for a man to be condemned by that law which he himself hath made, and to reprehend that in others wherein himself likewise trespasseth: to me therefore that ancient Law of Solon seems altogether unjust: wherein is said that if the man take his wife in adultery, let him kill her, but if she take the husband in adultery, let her not once touch him with her finger: for once that Law being recited amongst a company of matrons, one of them (courteously smiling upon the rest) said: I see plainly that women were excluded out of the council of men when those laws were ordained: for if there had been any woman there, they would never have suffered this Law to have passed so injurious to our sex.

Also that Law was unjust which was had in use amongst the Egyptians, as Diodorus maketh mention: for it appointed the man taken in adultery to be scourged or whipped: but the woman to have her nose slit and disfigured, to the intent she might in that part be punished, wherewith the face is most comely garnished to the sight of the world. Notwithstanding, in matters touching wiving there is nothing harder than to make a good choice, for maidens are brought up at home within doors, and do very seldom go abroad to be seen: for the which cause it is almost impossible for a man to search out their beauty, manners, and conversation, which matter surely maketh men doubtful what to do: for it is a thing of no small effect, to marry a wife and with her to frequent perpetual society of life, which in all points is unknown unto him at the first.

The manners and conversations of maidens cannot be better guessed at and perceived by any other reason than by the similitude or likeness of their parents: for it is very like that of good parents there can no evil children be gotten. A chaste mother bringeth up chaste daughters, and she that in heart never committed shame will not wink nor bear with any fault of her daughter.

All young men for the most part do desire to marry a fair wife: but yet it is (by the opinion of Theophrasus) less grief for a man to have a foul than to keep a fair wife: for he thinks that no thing is there safe which all men do desire, because some one man doth entice her by beauty, some by wisdom, and some through eloquence, and some by bounty and gifts, and that which is assaulted in every part is vanquished on some part. This much doth Saint Jerome discourse upon after the mind and opinion of the Philosopher Theophrastus.

Ennius the Poet said that we must marry wives that are of a sound chastity and which are seen to be of a portly favor. Aulus Gellius expoundeth this sentence and showeth that those women be of portly favor which are neither of the fairest nor yet of the foulest feature, but mean between both: which mediocrity surely is in all things best and chiefest: for this reason is sufficient to the procreation of issue: for pleasant beauty in the woman helpeth much, as in the men worthiness or dignity is most acceptable: these and many other things are to be thought upon in the choice of a wife, and namely this, that a man choose one that in goods and feature is like to himself: for inequality breedeth contempt and perpetual brawling, but equality knitteth together the minds with most firm love and affection. It is also good for a man to take such a wife as hath not been touched, nor married to another man before: for there is a double labor and trouble to him that marrieth a widow, first to unteach her the manners of her former husband, and secondly to enure and acquaint her with his own fashions.

Aristotle thinketh the best time for maids to be married at the age of eighteen years, and for a man at thirty and six years of age: for those aged are ripe and perfect for procreation of issue: but as touching the training of them up in fashions, if they were a few less years younger, I would think it more commodious, specially in this our time, wherein vices (as the Satirist saith) do swarm. Lycurgus also affirmed that it was a shameful thing for man and woman to pass beyond those years unmarried: for he ordained that those persons should be noted with infamy, and expelled the Theatres, who at the age of thirty seven years were found to have lived without a wife. The Romans also debarred all them from bearing any public office and esteemed them as unworthy to be honored any way by the common weale, which would not help and further the same with augmentation of issue.

Let the husband instruct his wife with the best manners, neither with threatenings, reproach, nor stripes: for it is a servile thing and not meet at any hand for familiar society: and indeed, wives become obdurate with beating even as naughty servants and bondmen become worse and worse, and with stripes are daily more and more given to follow their own willful ways. So women are less obedient to their husbands and do all things peevishly against the grain, when they are ungently entreated of their husbands, and getting at any time occasion for their purpose, running headlong into all filthiness without either awe or reverence of matrimony, thinking that they make none offense at all when they may lay for their excuse that they do it in revengement of their stripes before received: therefore with reason must we deal with them, that they may understand all things to be done for the common profit of their whole household, for the honesty of themselves and of wedlock. The secrets also that are and ought to be between man and wife, let them be included in the walls of their chamber and no further: for that man taketh an ill way both for himself and his wife's honesty which babbleth out those things that are to be kept in silence: for we must so cast our minds to live in wedlock, that we be not as a laughingstocks to any abroad, for any matters done without our own houses: therefore in matrimony all things ought to be kept secret: for what can be more lewd and shameful, than either the husband amongst his friends, or the wife amongst her neighbors, to chat and babble out such matters as ought in all points to be concealed.

Candaules King of Lydia had a wife upon whose beauty he greatly doted: neither thought he it sufficient to blaze abroad her feature and beauty unto all men, and to manifest unto the world such matrimonial secrets as were to be kept close: but also would have one to be a witness to his pleasures, and therefore brought her forth naked and showed her to his companion Gyges (as Herodotus saith) whom, as soon as Gyges had seen, he was so inflamed with love towards her that he thought upon, nay, cared for any other thing more than how to obtain her to his own will: and she throughly knowing the matter and supposing herself to have been of her husband thus betrayed as one that alienated his dealings and love to another, devised with the adulterer Gyges to murder her husband, and thereupon bestowed both her kingdom and herself upon the same Gyges. By this means did Candaules lose both his life and his kingdom, when he thought his pleasures to be less, so long as they were kept in silence and unknown.

Cleobulus Lyndius (accounted one of the seven sages of Greece) giveth us two good lessons touching wiving: the one is that we should deal with them by flattering; the other that in presence of strangers we should never chide them: for the one he said was a point of foolishness, the other of madness.

Furthermore, let the husband commit in charge to his wife all things domestical and within doors, and let him suffer her to have the dispensation of the same.

Let her perform her diligence at home, and let the husband employ his industry abroad: let her nourish and foster the children, and let him instruct and teach them: let the goodman of the house, as need requireth, know to seek after such things as appertain to the use of the family, and this not by usury or any other filthy lucre, but either with tilling the ground and fruits of the earth, which is never covetous, neither dissembleth with her tillers: but evermore restoreth the seeds to her committed, with most plentiful fruit and gain: fro it is meet and convenient that the common mother of all men should nourish and bring up her children, as it were, with dugs and increase, either with liberal sciences, or merchandise, or navigation, in traffic, in selling and buying, without lying or vanity, or in other honest trades, tending to the profit and ornament of the city.

Furthermore, it behooves him to spare and save that he getteth: for in vain do they take labor to get riches where is no regard of sparing, and where the expenses do still run out without any coming in. Neither is this proverb of drawing up water in a pitcher that is full of holes any other thing that first to get, and then prodigally and rioutously to lavish out. Yet would I not that the householder should be a miser and stained with pinching covetousness, than the which plague there can be none more pernicious, neither yet more discrepant or further from all humanity: for the covetous man hurteth all men, is odious to all men, neither doing good to himself or to any of his friends. He never rejoiceth at heart's ease, he is always sad, churlish, pensive, and crabbed; he only cannot find in his heart to love and cherish his wife and children, nor depart with anything unto them, to live merrily with all, but always is found a starver of himself, an oppressor of his own nature, is always hungry, always thirsty, and continually vexed with an insatiable greedy desire, neither can anything suffice him. Very aptly did the rich Attalus compare a covetous man to an hungry dog that snatcheth up fragments of bread and meat at his master's table, which slappeth up straightways whole and unchewed gubs without any taste, and straightways with open mouth looks still for more, standing at receipt of further hope for more to come.

Let a man thankfully enjoy his goods and estate present, and with well doing let him hope still for better: for it is the part of a fainthearted person too much to fear penury, and for that cause not to dare to use those things which are present: because (forsooth) he feareth that he shall hereafter lack.

The charge of all dealings within the house belongeth unto the wives: and it were very hard dealing that the goodman, who travaileth and taketh pains abroad to seek thrift, when he cometh home into his own house, as it were, into the port or haven of tranquility, after a most dangerous and hard voyage, should also be busied and troubled with ordering household affairs at home, when he, surceasing all care and desiring to be a quietness and rest, repaireth home for ease and succor. Therefore let the wife perform her diligence and let her take upon her the charge of all things which are at home to be ordered, according to the prescribed ordinances of the husband, unto whom in all points she ought to be obedient, for it goeth very ill in that household where the wife beareth all rule and the husband obeyeth and is made as one of the menial folk.

Let the wife especially set in order her household stuff and those necessaries that are neat and of value, which are to be reserve to the use of a better life, whether the same belong to womanly furniture or to man's apparel. Let her dispose and order them within secret rooms in the house that, whensoever occasion happeneth to occupy them, they may be in a readiness and not seek: for it is a most certain poverty, when a man lacketh that thing which he hath and standeth in need of the same, knowing not in what place it is laid up.

Moreover, such things as duly concern meat and drink, and which are prepared for dinner and supper, let he so daily dispense and bestow that they be neither wastefully gormandized and swilled up in gluttony and drunkenness by the folks of the house: neither by reason of too much niggardy and pinching let them be hungerbitten and starved. Therefore let her keep a mean, and so shall she at one and the self same time, both rightly provide for their health and also for the private affairs of their family, as well at one time as at another: and let her with great moderation qualify herself in those things which appertain to her own self, especially in apparel and ornaments for her own body, which greatly consumer her husband's substance: for they cost dear at the first and in small space are either by use clean worn or else sold for a great deal less than they were bought.

An honest mannered woman ought to fear nothing more than evil report: for she that once hath an evil name, whether it be rightly by her deserved or that she be wrongfully slandered, hardly can recover her good name and fame again: for a woman suspected of chaste living leadeth a miserable and wretched life.

The true ornaments of women are modesty, chastity, shamefastness, and praise, which cannot be purchased with any gold, pearls, or precious stones: but seeing it is so, that all these cannot be seen in any one good woman, although very honest: chastity yet is that only ornament which may supply whatsoever lacketh in the others: for this enlargeth the dowry; when it is not of itself sufficient, it not only adorneth and maketh comely that which is deformed, but also reduceth a woman to the similitude of beauty itself; it ennobleth ignobility, and finally fulfilleth all things which in any part otherwise be wanting.

The fifty Virgins of Sparta have eternized their names unto all posterity: for they being by their parents sent to do sacrifice among the Messenians, thinking to be entertained after the manner of hospitality, the Messenians with such impatience and concupiscence lusted after them, that despising the law of hospitality they sought means by soliciting their consents to carnal knowledge, and so to deflower their virginity: which filthy motion the virgins denying, and they importunately urging to dishonest their bodies, yet was there not one found of all these virgins that would consent unto their wills: but chose rather to die than so loose their maidhood, whose blood Lacedaemonias, through the great help of God, revenged afterward by a notable victory.

The second ornaments of a woman is to have pretty children, and of an excellent towardness: which ornament how much it is to be esteemed of, Cornelia the wife of Paulus Aemilius hath tuaght us: for when a certain woman of Campania coming unto her and showing out in a bravery her pearls, gold, and precious apparel, requested the same Cornelia in like manner to bring forth and show her ornaments and jewels, she fooded her out with words until such time as her children returned home from school, whom she showing unto the other woman said: Behold my delicate store and treasures, all mine ornaments, all my jewels and all my delights: which persuasion is the best that can be unto all matrons, that in respect of their children they should despise all other jewels and ornaments, and repute their chief attire in the hope and towardness of their children.

Besides this, let the wife take heed that she use no dissimulation, nor cloaked luggeling with her husband in any matter: for what thing can be more dishonest in a woman, than to show herself not to be the same which she was.

Pompeia the wife of Nero the Emperor was not only made a jesting stock to the world so long as she lived, because she pranked herself too much in curious trimming up herself to the best show of all beauty, but also purchased unto her name perpetual ignominy. For not Poets only, but Historiographers also, not a few do write that she not in a covert manner and classily but apertly and manifestly fancied this curiosity, and they affirm that she had always in a readiness, wheresoever she went, whole herds of asses that she might continually cherish her delicate fancy and rinse her mouth with the milk of them daily, thereby to appear the fairer and beautifuller: for there is no good hope to be had in that woman which seeketh to be praised abroad for her beauty. It was lawful for the Spartan virgins to go with their face bare till they were married, that they might thereby get them husbands: but after they were married they covered both their head and their face, as those then that sought after no husbands, but only cared to retain such as they enjoyed. But Gorgians Leontinus opinion is, that men's wives should be kept at home from going abroad: which thing surely liketh not me: but for them to go abroad very seldom, that truly do I greatly commend: for a woman that is a walker and a traveler from her own hous abroad, can seldom be chaste: let the wife show herself of one mind and concord with her husband in all things, for there can be nothing more pleasant among mortal men than when the man and wife do govern their household with concord and mutual goodwill together: and on the other part nothing worse than mutual discord and domestical brabbling.

The Athenians have taught us that silence in matters between man and wife ought to be used: for when as Philipp King of Macedonia warred against the Athenians, and that their scouts had intercepted letters of Olympias sent from her unto King Philipp her husband, they commanded those letters to be redelivered whole unopened and untouched, because they thought it was not lawful (no not for the enemy) to know and understand the secrets passing from the wife to her husband.

In wedlock also let all anger and stomaching be far absent, which makes love many times more slack and slow, and altogether diminisheth the same, disordering all domestical affairs and causing the state of wedlock to be more unpleasant.

The most ancient Romans did adorn that woman with a crown of chastity which was only contented with one husband and with continual widowhood, to profess and show forth the sincerity of her incorrupt mind: for she seemeth to be of an unbridled lust which marrieth again, especially if she have children, which are the pledges of matrimony and express the living image of her late deceased husband, both in continuance and name: moreover she that marrieth again is seen to be cursed and wicked towards her children, because they are deprived of their father and forsaken of all men: neglecting them as it were in the entrance of their life, even at the age and time when they have most need of their parents' help: which reason (undoubtedly) ought to persuade all widows to keep their chastity together with their children, that they make no further trial of fortune, of whom they being once deceived may scarcely home for better lot or fortune afterward.

Annia, a woman of noble race among the Romans, when her neighbors and friends persuaded her in her widowhood to marry with another husband, seeing she was yet of a lusty age and excellent beauty: made answer that she would not any wise so do: for, saith she, if I find a good husband as I had before, I will not be always in fear lest I should forego him: but if I should match myself with an evil husband, what need have I to try an evil man when I have once already had experience of a very good man: for she that is disappointed by the destiny of her first husband seems to be wise if she no more commit herself unto the fortune of marriage.

The daughter of Demotion the Athenian, although she was a virgin, yet hearing of the death of Leosthenes her espoused husband who was slain at the battle of Lenos, killed herself: affirming that, although she never had any carnal or matrimonial copulation with her husband, yet if she should be compelled to take another man, she should deceive the second, seeing that in heart she was married to the first: notwithstanding those women deal a great deal better who in the first flower of their years do hap to marry the second time, namely if they be then without children: for all living creatures desire to have and beget issue: and for procreation sake, rather than for lust to join together, seemeth a thing much more fir and reasonable.

Hiero of Syracusa, being on a time hidden by a certain familiar friend of his because his breath did stink, and he for helping thereof had used no remedies: said, that he never knew so much in himself before that time and blamed his wife, in that she had never admonished him thereof: to whom his wife modestly excusing herself, said, Husband be not angry with me, for I thought that all men's mouth's had smelled so, and therefore I kept silence. Armenia also coming home from a royal feast made by King Cyrus, when all men for the comeliness of his person highly praised Cyrus, she being demanded by her husband what she thought of the dignity and feature of the king: Husband (said she) I never turned mine eyes from you, and therefore what another man's feature is, I am utterly ignorant.

In the education or bringing up of children there are two things especially to be considered, whereof the one chiefly appertaineth to the mother, the other unto the father himself; the first reason concerneth the means to live, the second to live well: the first because it is and falleth for home, belongeth to the duty of the mother which ought to be the governess of the household matters according to the prescribed ordinances enjoined her by her husband. The matron therefore that is with child ought to forecast and consider that she must bring forth a child, and great diligence must she take that in no respect she hurt the child with her body before it be brought into the world, and especially she must cherish her own body and take her meat with modesty, feeding upon such kind of food as may nourish and strengthen her young one, and not that which may weaken it, and she shall shun to much sloth: a moderate walking for her is profitable and healthful, and causeth far more easy deliverance in childbirth. She shall also beware of all vehement labors, especially dancing, which thing by example Hyppocrates confirmed: for when a certain woman could not avoid the received seed of man, she desired his devise to help her that the seed should not prosper, whom he counseled: every day by jumping and dancing, to stir the seed. And so the seventh day by means of her leaping and dancing she brought forth an unperfect conception, covered over with a little thin rim or skin, such as we see is in an egg between the shell and the yolk. Some women keep such revel, rexe [wrecks?], and coil in dancing and leaping at banquets and feasts, that for very pain they either procure abortion before the time, or else bring the same forth very weak and feeble: others, to tend to seem pretty and slender unto their lovers, do gird themselves so straight that they hurt themselves and their bellies, also thereby very much: some cram and fill their bellies with dainty fare and wine, even till they surfeit again: and very many women use to cloy their stomachs with sour fruit and unripe apples. I let pass to speak of their lusts and certain beastly pranks, not by speech to be uttered, whereby they do not only travail before their time but also do bring forth into the world loathsome monsters.

After that the little infant shell be born, which not long ago the mother knew not because it was closed in her womb, let her with her duggs and with that fountain nourish and foster it, which provident nature hath with such plentifulness prepared in her breast. Worst of all (in mine opinion) do such women deserve of their children, which put their babes out to nursing, and that that time when they have most need of their mother's help, committing them unto young housewives and country nurses, such unto whom indeed some would not commit a young kitling, if they had any pleasure in it. Furthermore, they are not whole mothers, but rather appear to be half mothers, which straightway put out to nursing their own natural child and deny to give it suck, whom even now in their own womb, with their own blood they nourished: do they persuade themselves that their nipples and duggs are by nature given them for an ornament, or beautifying of their breast, and not to the nourishment of their children? But we do know some women with slibbersauces and medicines do dry up and stop that most sacred fountain, the nourisher of mankind, yea, not without great danger of their own healths, to the end (forsooth) they may appear the more beautiful and in the eyes of their lovers more pleasant and acceptable.

Let no good mother suffer her child to be infected with the contagion of milk drawn from another woman's breasts, and let her in so doing perform the point of a whole and entire parent, deserving well of her child: whom she shall thereby make more ready to requite and recompense her when it shall grow to further year's of discretion, if it shall perceive that it hath not at any time been defrauded of the mother's fostering and nourishment in the first beginning of life: for the benefit of the mother's breast was among the Ancients had in such reverence and regard, that whatsoever hard or difficult request the mother's were to crave at the hands of their children, their fashion was to request the same, for and by the milk which they gave unto them in their infancy and babeship. For what pleasanter delights or pleasures can there by than a young suckling child whose lisping speech and pretty endeavorings to bring out his words, his sweet laughter, and the pleasant mother's speech again used to her said child, seems to me far to surpass all other counterfeit scoffers or jesters.

Neither need apes or little dogs to be sought for there, to sport themselves withal, where little babes do creep about the house.

The members and tender parts of young children are to be fashioned by the nurse's hands, and the little infant's body to be wrapped and bound with a swathing band, from the shoulders even down to the ankle, but yet somewhat looser about the breast and bulk: for the breadth of largeness of those parts do very much to the dignity and strengthening of a man, and somewhat straighter about the stomach, and about the nether parts of the belly, the better to confirm and strengthen the same: and that the belly bear not out above comely proportion. Aristotle also affirmeth that crying is profitably given by nature unto children, for the thinketh that it is an endeavor or striving used by the child to his increasing, and that it helpeth much to stretch out the breast and heart strings: wherefore he prescribeth the nurse not to force the child from crying. Women conceived with child ought to have great care of themselves, lest that they be delivered before their time or miscarry in childbearing, which thing that we may have foreknowledge of, Hyppocrates teacheth: for either he saith that the infant moveth and stirreth in the mother's womb, upon the 70 or else 70 day, and it expresseth that it is either the seventh or ninth month, wherein she shall be delivered of her child, so shall a careful mother be skillful of her time of deliverance before it happen.

We must take heed (as Celsus saith) lest in time of prosperous health we do consume and waste away such things as should be safeguards and preservations unto us in sickness: wherefore a lusty healthful man, who is at his own disposition, will refuse no kind of meat that the common people useth, and twice a day rather than once desireth to eat meat: neither taketh he any less that will satisfy his stomach: he useth also diverse kinds of life, as sometimes to be in the country, sometimes in the city, but more often in the fields. To sail upon the seas, to hauk, and to hunt, and sometimes to take his rest, but yet most often to exercise himself: for certainly idleness enfeebleth the body, but labor strengtheneth it, the one hasteneth untimely old age, the other maketh a man to have a long and lusty young age.

We must deal with children by a little and little to teach them, even as when we would fill a vessel which hath a narrow mouth: for if we pour water fast, it filleth and runneth over: but if we drop it in by a slender funnel, we shall fit it top full. To praise the industry and diligence of children in their exercises, doth unto them much good, and to child them for their sloth is unto them profitable also: for, to be preferred before their equals and to be praised for well-doing by their masters, doth much sharpen children's wits and quickeneth their courage in all their studies and exercises.

The mother's discipline and correction, for children in their first tender years of infancy is very profitable, and maketh them more prone, docible, and apt to learn and compass greater studies. Now when they shall come to seven years of age, let the father take care of them and instruct them with a certain greater diligence, whose charge is to train up his children to live well and virtuously, than which discipline none surely can be more profitable or of greater effect given to mortal men. For Alexander, who for his wisdom was surnamed the great, was wont to say that he was no less bound unto Aristotle his schoolmaster than unto King Philip his father: for albeit his father had begot him into this world a living creature, yet Aristotle was he that taught him the way to live well, which knowledge h indeed thought was to be preferred before bare life.

The chief and special token of wit in children, saith Fabius Quintilianus, is memory, when as the child learneth easily and remembreth surely. It shall therefore be best in the first years of their youth to exercise memory for the more perfecting and throughly furthering the vigor and force of their wit, and either by ambition or rewards and gifts to allure them, to the end they may keep many things in memory and not be ashamed or abashed to utter and recite the same in any great assembly of people. For the propounding of reward and allurement sharpeneth the wit, stirreth up the memory, and maketh the minds of children more cheerful and prompt to any matter. There are some writers which suppose that blushing in a child is a very good sign of shamefastness, and better than paleness: for paleness argueth too much fearfulness, the other pretendeth and showeth a very good towardness, as Diogenes witnesseth: for on a time he seeing a child to blush, "Be of good cheer, my son," quod he, for such a kind of color is the color of virtue. If the father understand or perceive his son to be docible and of excellent wit, no covetousness ought to let or stay him whereby he should frustrate his son of so great a commendation: let him therefore so soon as he can betake his child unto good schoolmasters, that he may in those liberal arts be taught and instructed, whereunto nature herself hath most adapted him: for nothing ought more to be wished for unto the parents than to have their children learned, of whom surely to be vanquished and overcome in all kind of praise they ought not only to suffer and take in good part, but also to esteem the praise and reward of victory gotten by their children to appertain unto themselves.

There is nothing that causeth children to prove more obedient to their parents than when as they understand that they have profited in studies of good arts by the furtherance and diligence of their parents bestowed upon them: neither ought the child so much to consider of his parents' substance, which truly are but things transitory, frail, and in the hands of fortune, and which do only garnish and set out the body, but do not increase the mind or furnish it with perpetual goods: wherefore very well said Diogenes that a rich man being unlearned is as a sheep with a golden fleece.

Parents ought also to commit the custody of their children unto their friends to bring up, as well for that they do less cocker them being absent, and again because they will be the less wanton in other men's houses, being nourished at another man's table and cherished by another man's fire, and they greatly fear lest they should be very ill thought of and thrust out of doors by them, unto whom their parents had betaken and committed them in governance, upon great trust and diligence. For it hath been seen that even great princes, under tutors and overseers, have many times proved more excellent than under their own parents. I think it profitable for the child to be taught and instructed in two kinds of discipline at once, neither is it to be feared that the wit of the child should be overcharged by two schoolmasters of several arts or sciences: for he is put to no more painness, but his diligence is divided and tediousness removed: for when the child is weary of one kind of teaching, he goeth straight to another, even as it were unto a haven or resting port of his travails, and the inconstancy of those young years which hardly persevereth long in one and the self same thing is not altogether unprofitable. Nothing more famous can be given from parents to their children than the studies of good disciplines and sciences which are therefore called liberal sciences, because they make men free from all vile and loathsome lucre and from all voluptiousness and loose dishonesty: for they reduce and bring us to wisdom: than the which there can be nothing more excellent unto mortal men, by reason whereof we seem to approach and to be conjoined with the living God: the reward of which sciences, if there were none other to be had among mortal men, verily virtue only of itself is sufficient: which yet always is accompanied with renown and honor, even as the body is with the shadow. If it be so that children be somewhat of a dull capacity or otherwise less fit or apt to receive learning, let them be put to learn the practice of some other trades and occupations, especially such as come nearest in goodness unto learning, lest that they remain unprofitable by means of idleness and sloth: for true is that sentence of Marcus Cato:

> By sloth and doing nothing at all:
> Men learn to do evil, great and small.

Therefore, diligent and painful citizens ought to drive sluggish and slothful people out of their cities, even as the diligent bees do the drones or dors, which will not take pains for the common honey: and we must esteem as most holy that ordinance which Solon enacted, affirming that:

That child to his father is nothing bound,
in any respect of duty natural:
if that for him he hath not found,
some kind of trade to live withal.

But if all other disciplines and arts should be lacking, yet ought they to foresee and regard that their children be not brought up without rule of good manners: for it is far better for men to be without children and to be forever barren and bereft of all progeny or issue, than when men have children to bring them up evil nurtured or of lewd behavior. Epaminondas the Thebane, a worthy man and of great wisdom, never married any wife: which thing his friend Pelopidas reprehending because he left not the seed or succession of his valiantness unto his children, and therefore that in so doing he did ill provide for the commodity or profit of his country: Epaminondas thereupon (smiling) answered: take you heed, friend Pelopidas, lest you do worse provide for the public utility of your country, which may happen to leave such a son begotten by you whose life perhaps hereafter may be wished of some to be better: by which saying, this most wise gentleman showeth, that parents ought to fear nothing more than lest they have such children as may degenerate from their steps and qualities.

Neocles the Athenian, a man noble and excellent, had a son called Themistocles, whom in his youth he disinherited, because he was misliked and thought to live very lewdly, wasting his substance and in every point disobeying his father's commandment: this severe and hard dealing did not discourage the son, but did rather far more encouraging him to remember himself: for he thinking that such a manifest blemish of misdemeanor could not be extinguished without some singular industry and praise, from thenceforth wholly vent himself to the exercise of virtue, and by all care and study that in him was possible, endeavored to travail for the commodity of his common weale: and with all diligence that he could, protected and maintained the causes of his friends and private judgments: and within short space so amended his faults and reformed the vices of his youth, that there was no one man in his time preferred before him, and very few were thought to be found equal unto him: therefore the severity of a father towards such a son was not to be found fault withal, who indeed of a most naughty and lewd person, reclaimed him to be a man in all kind of praise most commendable.

Polemon, the Athenian living unchaste in his youthful years, was wanton and given to filthy behavior, sometimes also overseen with drink and having a garland (as the custom was for the stoutest drinker to have) rushed with his companions into Xenocrates school, only to flout and mock and to play some pageant of knavery: at that time as it chanced Xenocrates was discoursing amongst his scholars touching modesty, temperance, and chastity: which purpose for all this, he changed not, but plainly converted his meaning, even upon Plemon there present: by which oration made he so reformed himself, that without any more ado, forsaking there his companions and changing his former old life, he yielded himself scholar unto Xenocrates, and within short space excelled all his schoolfellows: and besides this, so nearly expressed his schoolmaster in all matters that after his decease this Polemon, being then left his successor, so learnedly behaved himself after the imitation of the other, that the schoolmaster was thought one style, and not scant perceived to be changed. Young men also are to be enured with bodily exercises, both for their better health, for (as Celsus saith) sloth enfeebleth the body, labor strengtheneth it, the one causing untimely old age, the other long and lusty young, and also for that they might be made more profitable members for the common weale in time of wars, wherein they are more prompt and active, if they come thereunto with a body exercised rather than by sloth effeminated: in which thing the Lacedaemonians did very much excel: whose children in running, leaping, and casting the dart were daily exercised and practiced: from whom Diogences on a time returning and going to Athens, was asked whither he went and from whence he came: I come (saith he) form men, and am now going to women.

BOOK 5

THE ENDEAVORS, TRADES, OFFICES, DUTIES, AND SEVERAL VOCATIONS. THE CIVIL CITIZEN AND THE UPLANDISH COUNTRYMAN. THE DISCOVERY OF VICES, WITH THE DANGERS THAT IN EVERY REALM AND COUNTRY THEREBY ENSUETH.

R APINE PROMISETH idleness and rest: but virtue showeth before her labor and sweat. Evil-mannered persons and such as in their speech and gesture be gross and unnurtured be termed uncivil: because they rather seem to have been brought up in the country than in the cities. From hence is derived the word and phrase of speech called *civility* or *urbanity*: because it doth appertain both to speech and manners, and is so called by the name of the Latin word Urbs, a city: because through civil companying or meeting together of wise and learned men, a certain knowledge and learning is gotten, which directeth and traineth up men in gallant courtesy, pleasant order, and comely grace, the contrary whereof is

If a man would in few words determine and define what a civil man is, he shall say that he is a good man, and one that is profitable to his common weale: for first and specially he ought to have before his eyes that sentence of Plato, where he saith:

> *Men are of God created, not only*
> *To profit themselves in this life present:*
> *But that they should their native country*
> *Study to profit with honest intent:*
> *Partly again that they be stillbent*
> *To profit friend, children, and kinsfolk natural:*
> *To this end to live well ought all men mortal.*

And by good right, human society is instituted and appointed to live together, for one to profit another. These things, when we shall consider upon, we shall well perceive that we ought to help and provide for our native country.

The little bees and ants, being creatures not only the least of all others, but also dumb and deaf, ought to be examples unto us, which undoubtedly do labor one for another: they swarm together, they keep themselves together, they are preserved together, with like defects and succors, they drive away their enemy with common danger, and maintain their store, their young ones, and all their company: for who can be counted a good citizen which is good for none but himself only, gathereth riches to serve his own turn without imparting anything to others, and scarcely for covetousness suffering his children and wife to have so much as may conveniently serve them meat and drink? For we ought to esteem the state of a common weale as a ship which hath need of the helping hands and diligence, of all them which are within it: every mariner ought to endeavor himself to the uttermost of his power, not only to save it from being overwhelmed and drowned, but also that she may arrive at some safe port or haven. And as in it, some holds the rudder or help, another directeth the sailyards, another looketh to the cables, and others about other matters as the case requireth, and they have alone mutual or common care for the preservation of the ship: so ought all citizens to work and travail, and some with council, some with diligence, some with riches, and some with painfulness and industry, to help the common weale, that not only it be kept in good estate, but that it may every day increase better and better: for those citizens that be thus minded are counted best, and by these means do they make the public weale most wealthy. For surely no riches, no revenues do more enlarge the state of a city and make it safer than when as the citizens among themselves be at unity and concord, and join together for the honor of their country. And on the other part, no power nor riches are strong enough where as the minds of the citizens are factions and jarring. Which thing Scilurus by a marvelous example taught: for he being by reason of sickness and age now come to decrepitcy, caused his sons being fourscore and ten in number, to be called before him, and holding in his hands a bundle of spear staves, which he had bound up together, in number so many as he had sons, wrought forth the same to every one of his sons severally, commanding them to burst them asunder, which thing they affirming to be unpossible, the old father drew them out one by one and burst them asunder all, and thereby took occasion to admonish them that while they agreed and were at unity among themselves they should not be overcome by any force or power, but that the longer they lived, the stronger they should be: contrarily, he told them that they should be weak and of no force if they disagreed and were at discord among themselves, and that every little enemy should the easily enough overcome them: for true is that ancient sentence wherein is said, that

> *The common weale is a continual living creature,*
> *Which is never killed, nor dieth at any time,*
> *Except to itself it injury procure:*

And be the sole causer of proper ruin.

The Romans possessed the Empire of the whole world, so long as they abstained themselves from civil bloodshed and intestine wars, but when the ambition of Cinna, the infamous table of Sylla, the bloody slaughter of Marius, and the wars of the son-in-law against the father-in-law enkindled and invaded the weale public, then the Romans (before the chief rulers of the world) became laughingstocks unto their rascal people, and unto their barbarous enemies: wherefore in a free city there can be no better persuasion than that which traineth everyone unto concord and unity, wherewith even the least cities are increased and enjoy the benefit of perpetual liberty: for this is a sure and safe wall of defense: these are the adamant towers which with no force, no warlike engine, neither with any thunderclaps of Jupiter, can be destroyed or thrown down. By this means shall this our citizen, whom we would have accounted very good, be minded to unity, if he following the opinion of Pythagoras and Plato consider that our mind doth consist in three parts, whose principality and reason they do show to rest in the head as in the tower or castle of the body, that this our mind being immortal should always be nourished with the food of contemplation of greatest and weightiest matters.

Let our citizen frame his mind to execute the talent or gift wherewith he is endowed: for the office of the mind is to use reason, which ought always to bear rule and to have our appetite or desire so inclinable and obedient thereunto that we covet not anything filthy or undecent: and even as an horse unruly and trampling is governed by the bridle and bit of a good rider, so let the appetite or affection of the mind be led by reason, to whom let him always obey and never obstinately resist if he desire to be accounted a good and wise man: for true is that sentence of Marcus Fabius Quintilianus:

As the bird to fly, the horse to run,
And wild beast by nature to cruelty
Are given, to live under the sun:
Even so, man hath activity
Of mind and wit to live withal,
As creature with reason imbued:
That tis believed, the original
Of his soul is celestial institute.

Fortitude, temperance, prudence, and justice are four sisters linked together in mutual bands; they are never separate, for surely one of them alone without the others cannot be perfect, but seemeth altogether maimed and unperfect. Fortitude without wisdom is counted rashness. Prudence without justice is deemed craftiness and an evil kind of malice. Temperance without fortitude is reckoned cowardice. And justice without temperance is thought to be cruelty. Whereupon Ennius the Poet saith: Sumum ius, sumu injuria: extreme rigor is extreme wrong.

Let therefore those four virtues agree among themselves in a concord, even as it comes to pass in music and instruments, that they may make a perfect concord, consonancy, and harmony.

It is common profit which maketh men to gain good report for their well-doing and well-deserving of all men, which the Ancients in time past so highly esteemed that they vouchsafed those persons of divine honors of whom they had received commodities and profit. For Hercules (though a mortal man) yet was thought to be in the number of the Gods, for no other reason but because he bestowed by many great commodities upon many nations: for either he bustled or contended with wild beasts destroying countries, or, with his arrows, killed the loathsome filthy fouls, or slew the perilous pirates and common robbers which kept the seas and beset the ways with such dangerous stales, that no travelers might pass, or else [he] did some other such kind of worthy exploits: doing therein much ease and profit to mortal men and making their life more safe and happy.

Dyonisius, also called Bacchus, was counted a god, because amongst the Thebanes he taught the use how to make wine and was reputed not only noble and famous in warlike affairs but a very good searcher out of hidden secrets, for he first played the Philosopher in Europa and then in Asia. So was Triptolemus honored for a God, because he taught the use of corn amongst the Athenians: and Isis a Goddess because she taught the order how to sow corn and flax. Therefore doubtless they are worthy of rewards and dignities, which do profit men with inventions.

It was the point of a noble mind not to permit in any wise that a man should deceive himself, which thing by a pretty example Carneades doth admonish us in this wise:

> If thou knewest a serpent lurking privily
>   Under a place, and wouldst have any man:
> Unawares to sit down even there presently,
>   Whose death might redound to thy profit, then
> Thou shouldest do very ill, except with warning
> Thou didst dehort him thence from harming.

A good man is always one and the same; he never swerveth from himself, and had rather be honest in deed than so to be accounted; he is not covered with any cloak of dissimulation, keeping inwardly privy hatred and heartburning, and yet outwardly pretending a fair face: but hath always one countenance, his eyes always after one manner, his look always one, and his speech in like manner always true.

A citizen must always beware that no notable vice reign in him: he shall exercise those arts and sciences wherewith he may be able to live honestly, without injury, and to bring up his family: for he ought to have regard of his domestical matters to the end he may help his children, kinsfolk, and friends: but especially the common weale of his country when time shall require: for as Cicero saith, the private possessions and riches of every man are the riches and wealth of the city. Let them gain, but without injuring or hurting of others: for as the Poet saith,

> Goods that are gotten by sinister means
> Are in like sort consumed again.

Architas of Tarent, a noble Philosopher of Pythagoras' sect, when sent letters unto Plato that he should beware and take heed of Dionisius the Tyrant of Syracusa, if he loved the safety of his own life: was had in admiration amongst all men, because he was skillful almost in all arts: this man was of such dexterity of wit that he made and framed by a certain wonderful reason and artificial workmanship the proportion and image of a dove, which dove, as Favorinus the philosopher reporteth, did fly: it was contrived with such equal weight, and in the same was a wind enclosed, which with a temperate spirit caused it to fly.

Amongst the noble praises of Affricanus, whereof both Polibius and other writers made mention: this one was accounted great, that he daily went down into the judgment hall and from thence did not return homewards again until he had gratified and done good to some one or other. And Titus the son of Vespasian (who after his father was Emperor of Rome three years) was of such gentle and courteous nature, that at supper time remembering that he had pleasured and done good to none that day, said these words: Friends this day have I lost.

It shall be the duty of a civil man to use liberality and frankness, in gratifying with requital and thanks unto others, and never to forget a good turn received: which respect of courtesy was so highly in the old time regarded, that not only persons living but even the very persons already dead could not neglect it. For Simonides the Poet, seeing as he journeyed, a certain man (unknown to him) lying dead and raised out unto the birds and beasts of the field, did straightway bury him, but when he came to the place where he thought in his mind to have taken shipping, he then again saw in his dream the same party whom he had buried, warning him not to enterprise his voyage as he had determined: for if he did, he told him that night he should suffer shipwreck: and when Simonides had told his dream unto his companions, they laughed him to scorn, and he alone remained on the shore, the rest of his other companions not crediting his words: but as soon as the ship was gone a little from the land, there arose a tempest incontinent that brake all their tackling and all to squatted their ship, that they were drowned every mother's son: and so Simonides, for the good turn that he did in burying the dead man, received thereby the benefit and safeguard of his life.

Let every good citizen take heed, that he be not found a blabber or liar in his talk: for to lie is the property rather of a servile than of a free mind: for Aristotle very prettily to a certain person, demanding him, what liars gained by their lying? answered: that they cannot be believed another time when they tell truth: but yet it is a far worse thing for any man to forswear himself: which fault was so odible among the Egyptians that all perjured persons suffered punishment of death as they which neither regarded religion towards god nor faith towards man. Let the honest citizen moreover bridle in himself a certain brainsick sauciness and brabbling in speech: for as it is a praise to speak lively and boldly if at any time a man have need to speak: so is it worthy of dispraise not to have a stay of the tongue if silence be necessary: for Cato, in his adolescence studying eloquence and philosophy, used a certain wonderful silence of speech, and when on a time a certain familiar friend of his said unto him: Cato, many men do find fault with thy silence, he answered saying: I will speak when I have throughly learned to speak such things as are not worthy of silence.

Pythagoras also the most wise prince of Italique Philosophy taught his scholars to be silent before he taught them to speak, thereby showing that a man's words are first to be premeditated or thought upon, ere they be uttered. For to bridle and restrain the tongue, which nature (meaning silence) hath walled about with a trench of teeth, is a point of no small wisdom: therefore the said Philosopher restrained talkative young men, enjoining unto each of them five years of silence.

Aristotle, when he sent his scholar and kinsman Calisthenes unto King Alexander, among many other precepts gave him this one: that he should use to speak very seldom, but yet very pleasantly before him, that had both the power of life and death in the sharpness of his tongue: such persons also as have diligently searched the natures of living creatures do write that certain living creatures lacking reason do maintain their safety with much silence: as geese which by reason of too much heat forsaking the east and flying westward, in their flight over the hill Taurus, where many eagles breed (which ravenous fowls they greatly dread) do use to fill their beaks with little stones, lest that the force of custom or necessity should move them to gaggle and there bewray themselves unto the eagles, to the great hazarding of their lives: but after they have silently passed the top of that mountain and hills thereabout, they let fall the little stones out of their bills, and with more careless flight hold on their course along the air with loud noise and far clearer voices. Let therefore the citizen learn to keep silence and to consider with whom he doth talk, and let him observe opportunity in speech: for sure according to the old proverb: A word once past cannot be called back. And therefore let them rather use the example of the geese [rather] than of

Calisthenes: for they by a little silence saved their lives, but this man even with a small liberty of speech lost the same, when as he would not give ear unto the saying of his good master: for greater is the praise of a seasonable silence than of talk out of due time used.

And furthermore, let the good citizen be ignorant in glossing and flattering: for neither can the glossers or flatterers in any respect profit either kings or princes. And true is that sentence of Quintus Curtius mentioned in his most excellent books of the Acts of Alexander, where he saith

More often is a kingdom spoiled through clawback's flattery
Than by main force of foreign foe, or homish enemy.

Aristippus the Philosopher did earnestly sue to Dyonisius the Tyrant for a certain thing in the behalf of his friend, which when he saw he could not obtain straightway he humbly embraced the Tyrant's knees, and by and by obtained his desire: and when this thing was laid in his dish for a reproach)by such persons as were present) he pleasantly said these words: I was not the author of this kind of flattery, but Dyonisius himself, who hath his earns in his knees: and Diogenes being demanded what beast did bite cruelest, merely answered,

Of wilds beasts a backbiter
Of tame beasts a flatterer.

For indeed flatterers do very much hurt not only amongst princes whom they do provoke to tyranny and cruelty, but also in a free city oftentimes (to creep into the favor of the common people) do give advice upon things which are against a common weale, and now and then make the foolish multitude of people stark mad.

Moreover, let not a good citizen be hasty or rash to anger: let him at no time speak anything in chiding mood or rage: for anger proceedeth of the weakness of man's mind, and that by a probably argument or reason is showed: because angry persons are, to them that be in good case, faint and cold, unto men they are women, to young men old men, and to persons in prosperity, miserable: yet notwithstanding many things are now and then done by anger, which, in the end (after the parties have paused and come to themselves) do make them sorrowful and repentant of that which they have said and done. Alexander oftentimes showed examples of an invincible mind, but because he was rash and hasty to anger, he emblemished and made his other virtues in some part more obscure: for he killed Clitus his friend being an aged man and guiltless: and a little while after, when he was come to himself again, he would have thrust the weapon which he took out of Clitus his wound into his own body, had it not been for his own friends that were then about him.

Dyonisius also the Tyrant (being on a time disposed to play at Tenys) laid down his coat and sword for a young man to keep, in whom he took great delight: here at a certain familiar of his (jestingly and thinking no harm) said: Dyonisius, thou puttest thy life into this man's hands; and the young man laughing at the same words, the Tyrant commanded both of them out of hand to be slain: the one because he had showed a way to kill him, and the other because he allowed and took pleasure at the saying: for the which act certainly he was afterwards so sorry, that he never took anything more grievously in all the days of his life. For in such kind of anger when the mind is kindled and enraged, we must surcease from all manner of dealings, till the heat of choler be assuaged, following herein the example of Architas, who being on a time somewhat moved with anger towards his servant, said these words: with what mind should I entreat thee, or how would I deal with thee now if I were not angry?

Demosthenes, that most excellent orator, seeing the nature and disposition of Phocion, which was of contrary opinion to all other citizens of Athens, said on a time to him: Phocion the Athenians will kill thee, if a madness once take them in the heads; to whom Phocion answered: nay they will kill thee, Demosthenes, if they ever chance to be wise. Furthermore a civil man ought so to dispose and frame all the ages of his time that in every one of them he may exercise himself in that which shall then best become him, neither let him do any such things in his childhood or youth whereof he may afterwards repent when he is grown to further years: on the other part to omit nothing which he ought to bring to pass at those years. For in childhood is praised that towardness of wit, which foreshoweth hope of honest life in time to come: in adolescency disciplines of good arts: wherein, who so excel, do seem presently right excellent men: then in the rest of the ages of man, the fruits of works are looked for: that is to say, some conformity of sayings and doings: again on the other part, a child is commended for simplicity, a young man for gentleness, and an old man for gravity: in which point there is much amiss even at those first years which are more apt for learning, which surely many in playing and lewdness do lose: for growing to bigger stature for shamefastness they are ashamed to learn, whereas rather they ought to be ashamed to be ignorant. Undoubtedly that is true which was holden as a proverb amongst the ancient learned men:

> So long as ourselves to learn we must employ
> As in this world we any life enjoy.

Yet notwithstanding there are some which will not stick to mock and flout men that are given to study and learning in that age.

Themistocles the Athenian, a most excellent gentleman, being an hundred and seven years old and perceiving that he must then needs depart out of this world, is reported to have said that he was very sorry that he must then die when he first began to taste of learning and wisdom: what then shall others do, whose life is far shorter and less exercised in studies of good discipline? seeing that he which had run beyond the bounds of nature did think himself not to have lived any longer time to that attaining of perfect wisdom.

The longest space of man's life which by his birth and death is defined, some have fun in long race and some in a short. Plato affirmeth that LXXXI years is the lawful bound and end of man's life: Solon affirmeth LXXX years jump, many threescore and fifteen, and some the threescore and tenth year: for they do divide our age or time of life by the number seven, whereunto Pythagorians attribute a certain perfection and do show that in every seven years some change and altercation happeneth in the bodies of men: wherefore they affirm that every seventh year of our life is dangerous, which the Grecians call κρισιμον, the Latins Iudicialem seu decretorium, judicial or decretory: and this do they show by this means. First because in the first seven years children's teeth fall out or do loose, giving place to other teeth coming up more fit and ready to chew the meat: and at that time the perfect pronunciation of their mother tongue is perfect and plain. In the second seventh year the soft hairs or mosiness in young springalds appeareth. In the third the beard beginneth to burgeon and grow, and is the full accomplishment of height in man's stature. In the fourth he beginneth to spread and enlarge in breadth and thickness of stature. In the fifth the strength of man is fully perfected and made ripe and able for the procreation of issue. In the sixth, man stayeth his pleasure and voluptuousness. And in the seventh resteth wisdom and eloquence, yet now his strength doth by little and little secretly decay. And in the eighth there is a certain concinnity or aptness of the virtues of the mind, which remaineth in the night septenary or seven years. Finally in the tenth by little and little he groweth towards his end.

Pythagoras said that fourscore years was the prefixed time for the length of life, and divided it in ages by twenty, alloting unto childhood twenty years, to adolescence as many: as many to youth, to manhood other twenty, and to old as as many, comparing man's life unto the four seasons or quarters of the year: as to the spring, childhood: to summer, youth: to autumn, manhood: and unto winter, old age. But Varro a most excellent Philosopher among the Latins thinketh that children's age continueth till they be fifteen years old, because so long they are impuberes: that is to say unhairy and not apt to generation, from thence till thirty they are counted young men or lusty youths, because the body doth grow lusty large and strong till that age: until the age of XLV they are called men, because at that age they are best able to defend and help the common weale wit harmor and weapons: till threescore years they are called grave and ancient, because then especially man's body beginneth to draw towards old age: and from thence until the end of each man's life, he affirmeth the fifth degree to reach: unto the which age who so doth attain he calleth them very old men, because then the body becometh unwieldy by reason of age: but Staseas the Neapolitane, an excellent philosopher in his time and a rare physician, determineth and concludeth man's life at LXXXIIII years.

We ought not to desire to live long, no not although the destinies do seem to smile upon us or to favor our petitions, by reason of the sundry chances of fortune and doubtful health of our body: for a certain wiseman, being demanded how long a man should wish to live, made this answer: so long as the commodities of this life be more than the discommodities thereof.

Thephrastus (as Cicero saith) was wont to accuse nature, for that she had given unto crows and harts long life, whose life was altogether unprofitable, and unto men very short and swift, who might benefit themselves and others if they might have time of life fully to drink of wisdom's well.

Possidonius, a notable philosopher, said that one day of a learned man's time was more worth than never so long an age of the ignorant: let therefore our civil man live very moderately and let his diet and tablefare be according to frugality and temperance: for intemperance and gormandize enfeebleth the body and dulleth the mind: for as temperance maketh a man long young and preserveth the body in health and good liking, so the other doth hasten old age before the time and maketh the body weak, taketh away color and cheerfulness of countenance: for it is true which was wont to be in this respect, even by the physicians themselves, that:

> Many more persons by gluttony are slain,
> Than are by war, famine, or any other pain.

For men not able fully to digest that which they receive into their stomachs are given to be of unlusty health, they are evermore sick, seldom whole, and soon come to their end: and furthermore there is no gulf or whirlpool which doth more swallow up and waste a man's substance than gluttony, which the more it is filled and feed, the more it is still an hungered, and the better it hath dined, the more more it studieth and takes care how to sup. There are surely no riches so large and copious, no household treasure so notable nor wealth so great, which in a small time are not swallowed up into the belly.

Diogenes, on a time reading in a paper set on the door of a certain riotous person that was driven to sell his house, merrily and pleasantly said these words:

I well perceived this building sumptuous,
Beset with wine, and cates so curious,
Would vomit out his master shortly
That kept such revelry through folly.

Gluttony doth not only waste and consume the substance, but bringeth very many gentlemen into servitude: do we not see that smelfeasts and jesters become perpetual bondslaves for their bellies sakes? Are there not many which as it were buy their dinner and supper not only with flattering services, but also with most vile and absurd offices? For whom it were a great deal better to feed up on the very mast and acorns shaken from the tree, and to live with wild berries and apples [rather] than at another man's table to be fed with peacock and the dainty acipencer. Surely greatly are they to be blamed which seek themselves masters for good cheer sake, forgetting the state of liberty.

Albidius, a certain citizen of Rome, devoured and consumed all his good or substance in eating and drinking, and finally even the very house itself wherein he dwelt, which was then even all the substance he had left, was by casualty of fire consumed and burnt: this thing when Cato heard of, he sportingly said: that Albidius had sacrificed his renaunts and fragments: by the which saying Cato quipped the gluttony of the said Albidius, and showed that thereby he was become an open prey and laughingstock unto fortune: for the thing which he could not eat, he burned. And that which he could not revel, devour, or swill, that had he committed into the hands of fortune to sport withal.

Exercise is called the best sauce for meat, and hunger is counted a delicate or dainty dish finely sauced, for the provocations of gluttony and curious cates and junkets sought for both out of the air, the heavens, earth, and the sea do not savor or relish better with an idle slothful person than bread doth with him that laboreth and is an hungered. Ptolomeus the king, wandering through Egypt and his shoulders having not overtaken him with victuals, being very hungry, did eat coarse bread (which he got out of a shepherd's cottage) greedily and with great appetite: swearing, that in all his lifetime he did never eat anything more sweet and delicate than that bread as. Also Darius flying from Alexander (being sore athirst) did with great lust and greediness drink muddy and troubled water, taken out of the next river, which was soiled and stenched with dead carcases thrown into it, saying that he never tasted anything sweeter in all his life.

A certain swilling drunkard given to gulling and quaffing was wont to say in sport, that he never thirsted because he did with oftentimes drinking prevent his thirst: but the civil man must expect and look that nature will require meat, which (by walking, laboring, and exercising himself) is to be provoked: by the example of Socrates the philosopher, who on a time walking, a certain man asked why he so did, he answered:

> *With walking, hunger but would I feign*
> *Good appetite, for my supper to gain.*

The ancient Romans, for no other cause, used to sup in their open courts and under the open air, but to the intent to show their continence and frugality unto the people whose care and study was not so great to pester their table with many dishes, as it was afterwards to their posterity: for the Epicure who was the avoucher and maintainer of pleasures, despised fine and dainty delicates, and filled the barks of trees which he used for dishes with herbs and apples, and would say that a man should feed upon homely meat, because they are the more easily to be had: for delicate dishes and exquisite broths are prepared and dressed with great care and excessive cost, and do make a greater grief and trouble before a man can find them forth than they bring pleasure in eating. Hippocrates also writeth that such persons as are careful for gluttony and bellycheer are never in sound health, neither can be long lived, and that their spirits are so encumbered with too much blood and too much cramming, as if they were wallowed and soused in the mire: and therefore they have no mind upon any sober or heavenly thing, but always frame themselves to think upon their dishes and how they may fill their bellies. It is a thing profitable so to dispose the mind with something that thereby at all times and seasons fruits may be had and reaped: for few things can be wanting for daily expenses unto a civil man, if he will have diligent care to look to his husbandry and the feeding of his cattle: a very mean diligence wherein Cato said did increase a man's substance. Neither ought any man to be ashamed to feed flocks of beasts or herds of cattle, for even most noble persons of all the ancient people afore time did use to feed and keep cattle.

Let banqueting be seldom haunted of a good citizen: for it is uncertain whether the same banquets purchase a man favor or displeasure: for although those that are bidden guests be bound to requite the same with like again, yet there are many which being neglected and unbidden do take disdain thereat, and practice against the same either reproach or injury: for to keep banquets or feasts is thought to belong unto kings, princes, and most wealthiest personages.

Riot and covetousness are two plagues which (as Titus Liuius saith) have oftentimes subverted and utterly destroyed whole cites and empires.

Let the good citizen keep a mean in his apparel and observe a measure in his degree and ability: for indeed, as it is a foul thing to wear ill favored and undecent garments, so is it subject to envy to wear that which is too gorgeous and fine, and especially when as a man's substance will not stretch to maintain the same, or whereas he being indebted to others braves it out upon other men's purses:

for in apparel this is to be considered that a man wear nothing but such as he may lawfully, and that it do not differ from the customable order and usage of his country. Let it be such as may become both the person that weareth it, his stock and kindred, his years and manners: for as fine brave apparel (so far forth as it becometh) doth add dignity and authority unto men: so nice, womanish, and riotous apparel doth not commend and set out the body, but discovereth the vanity of the mind. Adrianus Caesar herein purchased to himself praise, because he ordained that the senators and worshipful persons of Rome should not go abroad but in their gowns, except when they returned home from suppers.

All necessary expenses are to be restrained, as the charges of funerals, which bring no commodity to those that are dead, and are chargeable to them that are alive: and yet their fame and good report which lived with praise and honesty is not darkened with modest funeral ceremonies: but on the other part their funeral pope shall not make the memory of them to be famous among posterity whose life, having been loose and inglorious, hath left nothing behind them worthy of memory.

Cyrus king of Persia commanded by his last will and testament that there should be no other sepulcher or tomb erected for him than the earth only which brought forth grass and flowers, than the which there can nothing be found more noble, neither anything that may more beautify the grave. Surely methinks the reason of the ancient Egyptians is to be derided, whereof Dyodorus maketh mention, because they despising the time of this present life did call their dwelling houses, by the names of inns, as they which counted their harbors and lodgings for a small time, but most vainly and fondly they lashed out lustily and spared no cost in erecting of sumptuous tombs and burials: for they thought that the graves were the perpetual and everlasting dwelling places of them that died and were therein buried.

The Scythians (as Plutarch mentioned) did bury with their dead kings their butlers, cooks, yea, and harlots: to that end as I think that their kings should want no necessary service after they were dead: and certain countries of India with their dead husbands either burn or bury their beloved wives, or others whosoever they best loved in their lifetime. Oh a matter not only horrible in sight, but also to be spoken of, to kill a living man, because the dead man should not lack a friend or servant, when as indeed he can never want or stand in need of such who hath no feeling at all.

Little differeth from this madness of the Indians the people called Massagetae, and those called Derbites, which do kill their kinsfolk and friends when they wax old, or by any casualty draw near unto death, making thereat great solemnity and feasting, and there eat them together with other meat: and this they say they do because they suppose it to be the worst fortune that may happen unto men, to be devoured with worms.

Essedones, philosophers of Europe, which dwelling near to the river Danow, used to celebrate the funerals of their parents and neighbors with merry cheer and jocund rejoicing of their friends and familiars together: the dead corpses being mangled and mixed with the entrails of their slain beasts, they do feed upon and eat up in banqueting: but the heads or skulls of their dead bodies they keep to serve them instead of drinking cups, garnishing them with gold and silver.

Semiramis a queen of a most haughty and excellent mind, causing a sumptuous sepulcher or tomb for her to be made, wherein she would live after her death, commanded these words to be engraven thereupon:

What king so ever shall have need
of money, wealth, or treasure,
Let him pull up this tomb with speed
and take thereof at pleasure.

These words Darius the king, reading and thinking there had been treasures hid there indeed, commanded the stone of the tomb to be taken away, which, being rolled aside, he saw other words and engraved unto this effect and purpose:

Except thou hadest been a king covetous
of money: insatiable and desirous,
Thou wouldest never have broken up and violate
the graves of them that are extinct by fate.

This most excellent lady by a civil derision did thus taunt the vice of covetousness.

Sertorius, having won Thynge, a town in Maurisia where (as the inhabitants said) the noble sepulcher of Antheus was being of wonderful, yea, incredible greatness, gave commandment that it should be razed and thrown to the ground, and therein found a body of LXX cubits long (as Plutarch maketh mention) which he beholding marveled greatly thereat, and commanded that the same tomb should be straightway re-edified and restored, and greatly enriched the fame thereof, lest otherwise he should have emblemished his honor by defacing and violating so notable a monument.

BOOK 6

ENTREATING OF NOBILITY DEFINED BY THE OPINION OF PHILOSOPHERS. THE COMMENDATION OF THEIR BOUNTIFULNESS TOWARDS ALL MEN: HOW SOME ARE THOUGHT MEET TO SUPPLY FUNCTIONS, BY REASON OF THEIR ANCESTORS BEFORE TIME AUTHORIZED TO BEAR LIKE OFFICES. OF GOOD PROVISION FOR THE SUSTENATION OF THE COMMONS. OF SUCH AS HAVING HOUSES IN THE CITY AND ALSO IN THE COUNTRY, CANNOT BE SO CAREFUL, FOR THE COMMON UTILITY OF BOTH PLACES. THE DESCRIPTION OF THE VENOMOUS VICE ENVY. OF SEVERE JUSTICE UPON MALEFACTORS, INJURIOUS TO THE STATE OF THE COMMON WEALE.

HIPPODAMUS MYLESIUS, a man desirous of glory, a worthy warrior, and excellently well learned in the studies of good arts, purposing to write of the good estate of a common weale, first and especially thought it convenient and necessary to divide and distinguish the city and country in several: for it seemed unto him a thing very hard to compass, to make a common rabble and multitude of men gathered together within the walls of one city to live quietly together, except there were a separation made between them.

Therefore he distributed and divided the people into three sorts: one to be artificers, another husbandmen, and the third warriors: and he thought it good reason that the magistrates should be appointed and chosen by all these persons indifferently.

Cicero unto Salust, who taunted him as a new made citizen and one come of base degree, boasting himself to be of most noble descent, answered on this manner: I have by my virtue, worthiness, and service to my country shined before and given light to all mine ancestors, that if they were not known before they might yet of me receive a beginning of their memory: thou by means of thy lewd life which thou has led filthily hast unto thy ancestors brought great clouds of darkness, so that although they of themselves were famous and notable citizens, yet by means of thee they shall be brought into oblivion: wherefore do not thou object unto me men of ancient race: for it is better that I do flourish in mine own acts that I have done than to lean upon the reputation of ancestry, and so to live that I may be an original or beginning of nobility and an example of virtue unto all my posterity. For Cicero might well bring proof of the progeny or offspring of his nobility, because he was lineally descended of the Volscian kings.

Plato, wisest of all philosophers, and his followers (from whom Aristotle doth smally differ) maketh four kinds of nobility: the one was of them which proceed from noble stock and ancient race of honorable elders: the second was of them whose parents were men of authority, princes, or chief rulers: the third was of them whose rulers excelled others in any kind of notable praise or commendation, either at home or abroad in the wars: the fourth kind of nobility he maketh that which he showeth to be most excellent of all the rest, when as any man excelleth others either in worthiness, wisdom, or magnanimity of the mind, and leaneth only to the virtue of his own commendation. And this man he judgeth worthy to be counted noble, who not only other men's worthiness ennobleth, but whom his proper virtue and valiantness doth advance to honor and renown: but unto these four kinds of nobilities Aristotle added the fifth: that is of them which famously excelled in any notable discipline. And this did he by good right, for they thereby do not only ennoble themselves and their lineage, but likewise ennoble the cities and countries wherein they were born.

Juba the son of Juba king of Numidia, being but a child and taken prisoner by Julius Caesar, did follow his triumph into Africa: and although he had lost both kingdom and liberty, and also despoiled of his honor and dignity, yet he betook himself unto learning, and within a small time proved so well that he was counted amongst the best learned writers in Greece: and whatsoever nobility fortune had taken from him, the same did the discipline of good sciences more abundantly restore in him: whereunto also Hannibal gave himself, even in the desperate and troublesome broils of the Carthaginenses, and being somewhat aged in years did learn the Greek tongue and therein became so eloquent that he wrote the acts of certain Emperors and certain excellent books of the ordering of warfare and martial affairs.

It seemeth mete that they whose parents, grandsires, and ancestors have afore time been honored and endowed with public offices, should also have charge of the common weale, as it were by a certain rightful inheritance: and thereupon let them employ all their diligence and care: for as a field is very well committed into the hands of country born persons which know and can skill of the air and soil, even so they that are come of the race of senators have learned to execute those public offices, as it were, by natural discipline devised to them by their ancestry. For all the common people will be and obey more willingly and patiently their rule or authority, neither think they it amiss, for the son to bear office, when they call to mind that all his ancestors have executed the same office aforetime. They which bear rule in a common weale ought to have a diligent care, that the people be not oppressed, pinched, and famished with want of corn or graine, and that they may (as far as is possible) enjoy a perfect peace and tranquility: for surely all common people—although they be ready and prompt to revengement of wrongs, for the which it is seen now and then that they do enter into arms and wars—yet notwithstanding they expect some event and end, and if fortune favor them not they fall to brabbling with their rulers, by swearing, wresting, and turning all the fault in their necks: and moreover we must not rashly credit the opinion and rumor of the common people, for as Maro saith:

> *Scinditur incertum studia in contraria vulgus.*
> *The community unstable is dispersed in opinions variable.*

The opinions of which common people are slippery, wavering, and mutable, and not only for a day but not so much as for one hour steadfast and firm: wherefore it may be spoken of the common people which we do use in the proverb:

> *Of sand an infinite quantity take,*
> *And yet unpossible it is a cord to make.*

Religion, ceremonies, mysteries, and all divine honor whereby we make the living God merciful and at one with us, requireth men holy and innocent: who being endowed with the zealous study of sacred and divine scriptures, do wipe away the clouds of blindness and error from the eyes of men: for these men (to the end they may live modestly and keep in good order the temples and sacred houses, with great costs and charges edified) have need of wealth, riches, and fruits of the earth, which indeed do never or seldom fail, neither have they need to make any merchandise by buying and selling.

Without safeguards and defenders of the same, a common weale cannot be. For what should the citizens do within the walls if they had no other defense but within the walls of their city? In what wealth doth that city stand, or haw are the poor relieved there whereunto the husbandmen of the country do run for succor, when as in the fields adjacent there is fear on every side? In what hope, or in what diligence do the husbandment toil or moil, if they see their summer or harvest corn and fruits to become an open prey or spoil for the enemy? and without keepers give over all things in their fields unto fortune in every place?

The corn which is reaped in the common fields may be kept and reserved until such time as there happen a dearth or scarcity, or that the difficulty of war do urge in hollow trenches covered in chaff and very well fenced and made safe from all and every kind of vermin for seven years store, as Lucius Columella maketh mention: which thing surely, if it were diligently looked unto and that in his due season the old fruit were spent and the new fruit laid up in store, it should preserve the people from all siege and famine of the enemy: and with most safe and sure defense protect them from the annoyance of their enemies. For little prevaileth armor or weapons of defense in fight where the people do famish for want of sustenation: and a famished community is evermore studious and bent to newfangledness and tumult.

He that will have a well-tilled ground, let him sell his houses in the city: for he that taketh more pleasure of felicity to dwell in his house within the city than in his house in the country hath no need at all of any ground: for he cannot well handle civil affairs which taketh especial pleasure in husbandry and country dealings: for truly it cannot be but he must needs neglect the one of these twain, which coveteth to satisfy his mind with both these benefits.

Gardens planted with herbs and trees be made for pleasure and recreation: for in them are borders of roses, beds of violets, fishponds, and such other like commodities of pleasure: for grainers, barns, and storehouses wherein corn is laid, which do increase both profit and living unto man, do rather serve for the master's wealth than for his diligence: yet notwithstanding it shall not be impertinent for a citizen or civil person to have pleasure and practice in husbandry.

And as he groweth in more wealth to have many servants for the ordering of his husbandry, and such as be mere strangers born out of that country, unto whom he may prescribe the offices of that which pertaineth unto husbandry.

Strangers and foreigners, being merchants, are friendly to be entertained when they come into the city for good and honest purposes: for the societies and intercourses of traffic with strangers help the trade of merchandise among citizens and do make them wealthier and furnish the city with store of that which it wanteth, and carrieth away from hence those things whereof we have superfluous store and abundance: yet it is expedient that there should be but few of them denized with the freedom of the city: for certainly the multitude of inhabitants out of sundry places is dangerous in every nation: for the common people, gathered together out of sundry countries, seldom agree well, and there can scarce be unity or concord among men of sundry nations: and we may well so think that strangers will but a while continue in that zeal and goodwill, or natural affection, which freeborn people do, that have received from their ancestors, as it were, the seed of love towards their country, and have even with their mother's milk a tender goodwill and affection towards their citizens. Of the true citizens that may be spoken, which in lovely speech wives are known to complain saying:

A lover that already hath fixed his goodwill

Towards one, cannot be lured by good or by ill:
Enlist by flattering speech, nor urged to that end,
To change for a new, and forget his first friend.

So greatly is the love of our natural country engrafted in us, even by nature, that we cannot want or be without the same for any continuance of time or distance of places, for no reproaches, neither yet for any injuries. Therefore we must warily deal with strangers. For Aristotle affirmeth that all nations which retained many strangers and inhabitants of foreign countries to be resident among them were disquieted with discords.

We must especially take heed that nothing be done in the common weale by violence or fraud: for what things so ever are done by violence are weak and unstable, and not only provoketh the multitude unto envy but also unto revenge. Appius Claudius the Decemuir by violence challenged Virginia to be his bondwoman, which thing her father not suffering thrust his daughter through the body with his sword, and with imbrued hands returned to his host, exciting up the common people against the senators, which thing brought no small plague unto the common weale.

There by some that are sorry to see others surmount and excel in virtue: there was sometimes amongst the Ephesians a certain excellent man called Hermodorus, who excelling others both in learning and honesty was nevertheless banished out of his country: and unto certain men that marveled thereat and asked those people why they had banished so worthy man, they answered: there was no other cause but that in virtue and integrity of life he did to far excel the rest of his fellow citizens. For unto all good men doth [it] ever chance common backbiters and evil-willers: wherefore now and then we must dissemble if we desire to fly envy: assuredly wisdom must sometime give place unto rashness, for envy doth not only cast underfoot very many notable personages, but also doth subvert the state of cities, yea, and utterly destroy the cities themselves.

The poets fables of envy are notable, affirming that it is a plague feeding upon serpents: meaning thereby to show that envious persons do swallow poison and vomit up venom again: for another man's felicity is poison unto the envious person: neither can he take any joy of himself, except he infect others with his poison: and certain there can be nothing more filthy or more unfitting a man than to rejoice at another man's evil and to be vexed or ill apaid for other men's good fortune, both which things the envious man useth to do.

Tymon the Athenian did once make an oration at Athens in a great assembly of people, in the which he said that he had one only little orchard wherein was a great fig tree, upon which many citizens had hanged themselves, and because in that place he purposed to build a wall, he said he must needs cut down the same fig tree: and that therefore he was come to tell them, that if any would hang themselves, they should make haste and come quickly, while the fig tree were yet standing.

Every man maintaineth his private substance although it be small: neither doth the poor man less esteem of his small pittance than the rich of his great wealth: and if any contention happen to arise between a poor man and a rich man, although the rich man (indeed) be wronged, yet because he is mightier and wealthier, it will be thought that he doth the wrong and injury, and thereby purchaseth the envy of many others. But yet if any man do say that the poor man's patrimony is taken from him by extortion and violence or strong hand, ever man begins to fear his own case, dealeth newfangled alterations, raileth at his betters, favoreth the oppressed, bendeth himself unto seditions, and can never be quiet in his mind till he see that he hath safely and warily enough provided for his own safety.

Periander practiced tyranny in Ambracia and customably committed buggery with a certain boy, whom on a time as he was drinking in presence of many others, here merely asked whether he was at any time great with child by him or no: the boy was throughly enraged with anger and could not abide that those filthy things which he had suffered before should have been once named and spoken of: and thereupon found he means to kill and destroy this tyrant. Pausanias also of Macedon, a young man in beauty and nature most excellent, was likewise violently and forcibly abused in his body by Attalus, and by him was made drunk with wine and brought in at a banquet, and offered as a common strumpet unto the lust of the guests there: Pausanias stomaching this shameful villainy told the whole matter to king Philip, but the king with sundry delatory words seemed to have thereof no care, but rather made thereat a laughing game, preferring Attalus to better place and room in warfare than he: which injury so throughly touched Pausanias that he converted his displeasure towards the king and the revenge which which he could not take of his adversary, he extended upon the unrighteous judge: for as he sat at the marriage of Cleopatra the daughter of Attalus between both the Alexanders, the son and the son-in-law, Pausanias slew him, fearing no such matter, and by killing the killing turned into sorrow and heaviness that day which should have been a day of joy or gladness, plainly hereby showing that the complaints of subjects are not to be disdained nor contemptuously be rejected.

It goeth not well in that common weale where a man must live by prayer or entreaty, where citizens must live in that case that they dare not speak frankly or boldly those things which they think to be for their profit. Philip king of Macedon, under a certain pretense of liberty invading a great part of Greece, besieged Athens, excusing himself by letters and ambassadors, set unto the senate and people of Athens that he did not those things to the end he would take away from them their liberties or franchises, or to bring the city into bondage, but because he had a grudge against ten of their citizens, which in the senate house had always barked against him and did not cease to rail upon him with reproachful words: and therefore if those few might be yielded unto him, he said he would raise his siege and depart, and deliver the people from war and famine. Namely and especially he required to have that most excellent orator Demosthenes delivered unto him, upon whom all the countenances and favors of the Grecians were at that time bent and cast, and besides him nine others of the eloquentest and notablest persons both for talk and authority: hereupon the senate was in great perplexity and many of them agreeing upon this point cried out, that it were much better to save a multitude than a few persons: these few were shrewdly afraid, whom the king had requested thus to be yielded into his hands to death, and scarcely durst they speak their minds, seeing that by their deaths all the residue hoped for peace and liberty, and it had come to pass indeed that these few had then been yielded, had not Demosthenes displayed the craft and deceitful fetch of the king by this wittily devised fable uttered unto them:

> The wolf on a time (saith he) persuaded certain shepherds (whose diligence he had desire to deceive) to enter friendship and amity with him, conditionally that the shepherds should deliver unto him (as hostages or pledges) their dogs which were his hateful enemies, and gave all cause of all the strife and debate: the shepherds gave ear unto this tale, assented to his request, and for better assurance of their faithful meaning, delivered the dogs, which were the most diligent guarders of the sheep: then

the wolf, when all fear was taken away, not only at his fill but also at his pleasure devoured and tare in pieces the sheep, and killed the shepherds themselves. Even so (O ye Athenians) doth Philip the king at his present mean and go about: who desireth to have all their heads under his girdle which have impugned his doings and which do manifest and bring to light his secret treacheries and colorable dealings: because he may the more easily invade and sack the city, when it is bereft and spoiled of the safeguarders thereof: for doubtless the city must needs perish, whereas men may not speak their minds freely in such matters as concern the utilyt of the weale public.

Let the good citizen greatly abstain from civil blood, being ever mindful of this tragical sentence:

> *Whosoever he be that doth rule or reign*
> *From shedding of blood let him abstain.*

But if necessity constraint and that the city cannot otherwise be set in good state except by shedding of the blood of some naughty lewd person, let them deal as good physicians use to do, who after that they do plainly see that the troubled and infected members of their patients cannot by any manner of remedies be restored to perfection or recover, although it be against their wills and to the great grief of all the whole body: yet do they not let to cut of the same corrupt members, lest they should infect all the rest of the body: for we must not favor or spare any person thereby to bring ruin or decay to the whole common weale: but we must use revenge that the same may be preserved in safety.

A mischief new hatching and but now in the prime,
Is soon to confusion suddenly brought:
But that which is old, and lasted long time
Is often incurable, though all measures be wrought.

To give as spoils unto the common people the goods of such as be proscript and out of the prince's protection is against all equity, and therefore the community of Rome deserved great praise and favor when Marius and Cinna proponed the richmens' houses to be spoiled by the citizens: for there was no man found so needy and so bare which at that time spared not from despoiling and purloining of that which another man had sore sweat and labored for. Neither was there any man amongst them which could find in his heart to reap any commodity unto himself in the time of that civil sorrow.

As severity in a city is sometime wholesome, so cruelty is always pestiferous: for the severity of Lucius Sylla was a beginning of all evils amongst the Romans: for that same most infamous table wherein were fourscore thousand persons proscribed, and of them four that had born the honorable office of Consul, to wit, Carbo, Marius, Norbanus, and Scipio, and amongst them also at that time Sertorius (a man in those days greatly feared) wrought much mischief unto the common weale: for other men, taking hereat example, in a small time subverted the whole Empire.

But yet the multitude of people, yea, though they do somewhat trespass, must be mercifully spared: Julius Caesar after that he had vanquished the host of Pompeius the great spared the citizens: and them whom he had by force of arms subdued he rewarded with benefits bountifully: and glorying in himself wrote letters unto his friends at Rome, therein mentioning that he took great and most sweet pleasure because he had preserved in safety those citizens whom he always reputed for his adversaries and enemies, and had made them to become, as it were, bound in tender affection and goodwill towards him.

The nature of cruelty doth make the praise of victory far less: for greater had the praise of Octavius been towards Antonius if he had not commanded [that] Attilius, being then but a child most innocent and the son of Antonius and of Fulvia, to be beheaded: and yet notwithstanding, Octavius straightway showed the evident tokens of repentance, for that which he had done: for he straightway revenged the death of Attilius: for Theodorus, the schoolmaster of the child who betrayed him unto Octavius, privily took from the child when he went unto his death a precious stone which he wore about his neck, whereof Caesar having intelligence commanded the same Theodorus to be condemned and hanged upon a gibet, and so revenged the villainy of that traitorous varlet, showing there in plain proofs of his changing mind, relenting in that which he had afore done.

No man can patiently brook to be flouted, contemned, and to be had in derision: for we read of Manlius Torquatus, the son of the most valiant and noble Lucius Manlius, was even from his childhood of a dull and blunt wit, insomuch that he was sent away by his father into the country as one that seemed neither fit nor profitabl, either for public or for private offices: but he within a small time after, as one weary of his slothful life, delivered and preserved his father being accused from a great a weighty matter of a judicial controversy: and in the battle fought by the Latins brought away the triumph and victory, to the great rejoicing of the people of Rome. Neither may Themistocles be pretermitted with silence, whose lewdness of life his mother dispairing (for the amendment or reforming) hanged herself: but when he came to be of more discretion, he proved himself to be of such excellency in all his doings that Cicero, the most excellent orator, called him the prince of Greece.

The age of twenty and four years is lawful and allowable for any man to aspire and attain unto an office: and let no man therefore [offend himself?] if he be not a magistrate before those years: moreover let no man disdain that any more ancient person than himself is preferred in office before him, both because the envy is greater among those that be of equal vocation and also because every man doth hope when he cometh to that age that then he shall attain unto like preferment.

It standeth with the honor of the city when the citizens are called by honorable and goodly names: for an uncomely manner of nomination or terming of them seemeth so to take away somewhat of the dignity of the person, as an honest or decent calling of a man seemeth to add worship, honor, or dignity: in which thing the diligence of the parents in naming their children is to be praised, and especially seeing that in that point they bestow no cost, and yet do not a little adorn their children therewith: wherefore some are worthy of dispraise, who, having parents and ancestors ill named, would never leave or digress from the same names, even as if they were loath to defraud their posterity of the reproach of ignominy of their ancestors.

Book 7:

THE NATURES, USES, PROFITS, AND CHOICES OF ALL SORTS OF GROUNDS. THE SUNDRY DISPOSITIONS AND INCLINATIONS OF PERSONS, ACCORDING TO THE QUALITY OF THE SOIL WHERE THEY BE BRED. THE COMMODITY OF WOODS, AND THE ORDERING THEREOF. THE GREAT NECESSITY AND BENEFIT OF WATERS, FOUNTAINS, AND SPRINGS, WITH THE STRANGE VIRTUES OF SUNDRY WELLS IN FOREIGN COUNTRIES.

MARCUS CATO said that in buying of lands two things especially are to be considered: wholesomeness of air and plentifulness of the soil: whereof if the one were lacking, he judged that that ground was not to be [accounted?] of and to be tilled. And not without a cause, for he that buyeth barren ground and fruitless soil buyeth to himself and all his posterity after him poverty and perpetual labor. And he that buyeth ground situated in a pestilent air, buyeth unto himself and to his succession continual sickness, untimely old age, and hasty death. For fruitfulness of the ground doth not a little further and help toward living well and pleasantly. Whereupon the

Arabians are called happy, because they abound and are enriched with corn, fruits of the earth, vines, and sweet odors.

Good choice must be had for the building of any city, that it be set and builded in a very wholesome place, and that is, if it stand upon somewhat high ground. For champane and plain ground is seldom in every point found safe, valleys are subject unto fulsom fogs and dangerous mists, but this high place shall neither the hot regions of the air, nor those that be too much cold and frosty, but those that be temperate prosper towards the east or towards the south.

Except it be such a country as is near the sea, for that hath commonly the southern and western winds hurtful, especially if there be any ground near fenny ground near thereunto, which have not their course and issue into the seas or rivers: for out of the standing water, so soon as the morning gleams of the sun appeareth upon the same, there ariseth cold winds or dampish clouds, infecting the spirits of the cattle feeding in those fenny places: with the contagion of that foggy mistiness, they do also infect the place and make it pestilent, especially in summer and autumn, what time the southern parts of the world be far hotter than at other seasons. Albeit all fenny and marshy soil is to be eschewed and shunned, because it always venteth out a most poisoned air, being in summer darkened and dimmed with vaporous fogs, and in winter with cold exhalations and mists: moreover by reason of fervent heat it engendereth gnats and other stinging and odious vermin, which do at such times flock together in swarms and infect the city, and be very noisome both unto man and beast.

Many writers do agree in opinion that Italy of all other countries is most temperate: and even as the planet Jupiter, having his course in the midst between the most hot and fervent planet of Mars, and the most cold planet Saturn, by reason of diversity in qualities receiveth temperateness, so it, stretching and lying between the north and south, receiveth a temperature nurture: therefore innumerable praises doth this country deserve, as Marcus Vitruvius saith: for in bringeth forth men of body and manners in proportion most excellent and which in fortitude of courage, wisdom, and discipline are able to surpass all other nations. Let the ancient Romans be witnesses herein, which with their warlike forecast and prowess tamed and daunted the outrageous fierceness of all the barbarians, and which (as Cicero saith) by their own industry either invented all things better than all the other nations, or else whatsoever they received of other countries the same they made much better and perfecter. And in small time they subdued all nations and obtained the jurisdiction and Empire of the whole world.

Natural philosophers affirm that some bodies brought out of cold countries into hot regions cannot endure and continue but are soon dissolved. Contrarily, persons brought out of hot regions into cold and northernly countries are not only not hurt, endamaged, or diseased by the change of the iar, but are made more lusty, healthful, and longer lived. Aristotle witnesseth that those people which inhabit cold countries do rather abound in courage, stomach, and strength of body than in wisdom or knowledge, and that their bodies are far taller and fairer: the same country people are also of a white complection, of a straight flaxen hair, gray-eyed, and full of blood, gross witted, but very mighty and strong, venturous and without fear, but in time of sickness they are fearful and fainthearted: as the Frenchmen, which because they excelled in largeness of body derided and scorned the hosts of the Romans, saying: Lo, what little fellows be yonder, of so small stature: of whom Caesar maketh mention in his most excellent commentaries, where he saith: the short and low stature of our countrymen was had in contempt amongst the Frenchmen in comparison of the largeness of their own bodies: and a little after as touching their wit he addeth thus: as the Frenchmen are ready and courageously minded to take wars in hand at the first, so if their mind very tender and nothing able to resist adversities. But contrarywise, men born in the south parts and being more subject unto the heat of the sun are less of personage and slenderness of stature, of brown or swart color, curly haired, black-eyed, their legs crooked and bending, weak and nothing strong: for these men, by reason of their small store of blood and subtlety of the air, do excel in wit, and are notable ingenious, wherefore they do quickly conceive and attain the knowledge of things, and are more prompt for devices and cogitations: in sickness they do show themselves to be of a right stout stomach, but in battle very dastards and cowards.

Cato distinguisheth a good ground by nine several differences. The first he saith is, where vineyards may bring forth abundant store of good wines: the second he appointeth for an orchard that may easily be watered: the third for osyers: the fourth for olive trees: the fifth for meadow: the sixth is arable ground, apt to bear corn: the seventh for woods that may be felled and lopped at their increase: the eighth for shrubs and bushes: the ninth for woods that beareth mast: for it must needs be a good ground which hath the more part of all these commodities.

The juniper trees do with their berries nourish the winter fowls, wherewith also capons being fed and crammed do nowadays furnish out the tables and make the same more elegant: and the wood thereof being burned sendeth forth a sweet smelling smoke and odor most wholesome in summer to expel and drive away all evil and noisome airs.

No man can deny but that the mast of chestnuts is profitable: for it is not only good for beasts to feed upon, but also for a man's whole household. This nut is so covered and harnessed, as it were, with a prickling shell that it can scarce be taken out of the same without hurting a man's hands: and therefore the country people were wont to bury the same certain days in pits or holes within the earth till such time as the uttermost pile of the nuts opened of itself, and so out of every shell there cometh two or three kernels. This tree groweth very big and is profitable almost in every respect for building: and of it are made very good tubs, and wine or oil vessels, which the carpenters of our time do call the queen of all trees, because it is counted good almost for all purposes and uses: whereof not only for fruit and wood, but also for timber it is to be accounted a chief and special wood.

How necessary fire is not only to the nourishment of man's life but almost unto all uses, every man may easily judge: therefore very ill should any choice of habitation be if it either stand far distant from woods, or altogether lack the commodity thereof. For we have read and seen in our time that cities by the enemy besieged have been forced of necessity to yield for default and want of wood.

Therefore that country soil is to be chosen for habitation which aboundeth with firewood, which is so to be used and appointed that every seventh year part of the same trees may be cut down and lopped, and that there may be enough to suffice the use of all the whole people: for that which is cut down had need to have seven years growth before it be cut again, that the young sets and shrubs thereof may grow fresh again, to their full size and skantling.

The wood which serveth for timber to build houses and ships withal must more diligently be looked unto, preserved and kept, and to be cleansed every year from thorns, briers, and brambles, that they hinder not the new griffs and springing plants from growing to their full height, size, and bigness.

At the spring of the year, trees do burgeon and bestow all their sap and strength upon bows and buds: and therefore become they weak and exhausted, as the bodies of women that are great with child are feebler, weaker, and slenderer of strength than others, and when their time of labor or childbirth cometh they become for a time unwieldy and weak till they have with good caudles and nourishments recovered their former strength again.

Even so trees, while they burgeon and bear leaves, and afterwards while they nourish their fruits yet unripe, are of less strength and force: but when in autumn their fruits or berries are shaken of, and that their leaves do fall, the roots do take again unto them all their whole sap and strength, and are so restored unto their former perfect solidity.

Thales Milesius preferred water as the principal of all other elements: for man's nature can easier bear with the want of anything than of water: for admit the corn fail and be not to be had, yet the profitable increase coming of young sets and trees may supply and administer sufficient provision wherewith to sustain life. We may defend life with flesh, by hauking, by fishing, with herbs and roots: but where water is wanting there can no food neither be had nor preserved fit for man's sustenation: and therefore we account that country altogether unhappy which either lacketh water or hath water unwholesome and corrupt.

Moreover, it was a manner among the Egyptians and of them very straightly for a long time observed, that before all the houses and temples of their gods there should be set a pot with water, to the end that they that went into the temples might therewith be sprinkled, and falling down to the ground with their hands (lift up to heaven) might give thanks unto the majesty of God, who had bountifully blessed and relieved them with most wholesome water. And furthermore, we read of certain countries by means of waters only ennobled and made famous, as the mountain Thiliadus amongst the Molossians, which Theopompus extolleth and saith had an hundred bridges. Magnesia is counted far more famous, by reason of the excellency of a well which the poets do there testify to be dedicated unto the muses, because whosoever drank out of the same became thereby sweet breasted and clearer to sing. Neither is it to be marveled at, forasmuch there be found innumerable virtues of waters, partly by apparent and partly by secret and obscure reason: of the spring in Arcady, which the inhabitants called Clitorius, which maketh such as taste of the liquor thereof straightway to abhor all drinking of wine forever.

Vitruvius saith that there is a well in Pahlagonia which seemeth as thought it were mixed with wine, insomuch that they which drink thereof are made drunk: the like nature and quality the river Licesius in Thracia is reported to have, on the banks whereof many times the travelers and wayfaring persons are found drunken and sleeping. The city of Ephesus also hath springs, not far from it, the waters whereof seemed mingled with vinegar, and therefore are most acceptable unto sick persons. And Strabo the geographer writeth that there is a water at Hieropolis so apt for dying of wool that if the roots of herbs be steeped and mixed therein, it maketh as orient and glorious a color as if it were scarlet or purple.

There be also which write that at Tharsis, a city in Cicilia, is a river called Cydnus, where persons that are bathed and a certain time washed, are eased of the gout. Moreover, Omponius in his cosmography writeth, that one of the two islands called Fortunate is notable and famous through the singular virtue of two several springs, of whom who so tasteth of the one cannot but laugh continually, and the only remedy for them that be in that case is to drink of the other. There is also another spring at Susi, in the country of Persia, which looseth and shaketh out the teeth of those that drink thereof: but to such persons as do wash themselves therewith it is most wholesome: and so they say there is a lake in Assyria, near unto the which groweth a slimy, glewish, and bituminous pitch of earth, of the same quality: whereupon, if a bird light, she is straightway limed and tied fast from flying any further. This kind of liquor, if it once be set on fire, can never be extinguished nor quenched, but only by throwing dust thereupon.

All hot waters have a medicinal force and virtue above other waters, although they be of their proper nature cold: but because they do flow or have course through the hot and ardent veins of the earth, therefore they come for the warm, which notwithstanding cannot long remain so, but be in short space cooled: for if by nature they had heat in them, they would not so soon become cold.

And surely unto me it seemeth a thing wonderful, that there are waters ordained by the providence of God, medicinal and able to cure all diseases incident unto mortal men, which do not in their curing vex the diseased persons with slyersauces, receipts, drugs, and bitter dilutions, neither torment them with fire or tool: but with a most sweet bath and washing do restore them into their pristinate health. Neither have the springs, which rise from sulfurous or brimstoney soil, these virtues only: but those springs also, which pass and have their course through allomy soil, which doth cure the lask and resolution of the sinews: they are very good also for them that have ill digestion and ill stomachs. Finally, they do perform that thing which Asclepiades said was the office of a right good physician: that is to say, to cure safely, speedily, and pleasantly: and bituminous waters also have their virtues: which rather by drinking than by bathing do help the diseased persons, for they do make the belly soluble without any pain or grief, and do cure almost all the inward diseases of the body by purgation: and sometimes the painful wringing of the entrails and guts, when they be exculcerated, and when that excoriation or bloodiness floweth from them, are thereby restored unto their former health.

There is also a nitrous kind of cold water, the drinking whereof doth purge and diminish all unnatural accesses of the body and specially the humors or swelling of the throat or the kings evil: such allomy and saltish nitrous springs yield forth for the most part an evil smell and relish: for their original, being from the very lowest part of the earth, do pass through the hot ardent veins of the same.

Those that have written of husbandry do say that every kind of pulse, being cast into water and set upon fire, doth try the same water very well, they be quickly and speedily boiled. Certain of the ancient physicians affirmed that kind of water to be best which is lightest, or else, which being set on the fire, will soonest be hot, so that it be clean and pure and unmossy. All water that is fetched from the moorish or fenny grounds is unwholesome, and so is all that doth not run but standeth still, or else that which runneth through shadowy places and dark canes, where the sun giveth no shine: but worst of all is snow or ice water, as certain ancient writers have holden opinion. Cornelius Colsus doth thus write of waters: rain water is the lightest water that is: next is spring or well water, then river water, and last of all is pit water. Then describeth he snow or ice water, and that standing water is heavy, but the heaveist of all others (saith he) is that which is taken out of a moorish or fenny ground. He that throughly considereth the nature of these things will willingly provide wholesome liquor for the use of himself and his fellow citizens.

The best situation for a city is that which is not far distant from the sea or from some great and navigable river, through which may be transported and carried out those things whereof we have to great store, and such things may be brought unto us, whereof we stand in need. Surely the mouths or entries of rivers have great opportunity [with? by?] their flowings and pleasant tides, do not only increase pleasure and become wholesome for all cattle, since they may go easily without any coursing and vehement resistance of the water, but also do make the fields and pastures thereat adjoining more rank and fruitful. There is great diversity in rivers and every of them hath not commodity alike: for the river Nilus is counted the most fertile and fruitfullest river of all others. It floweth through Egypt with great fertility: for when it hath an overflow, the whole land of all the summer time it goeth back again into his channel, and leaveth the fields fatted with mud and very fruitful for any tillage, insomuch that the inhabitants there have scarcely any need of the labor of oxen or of the help of any husbandman to manure the same any further, than only to cast their seed thereupon. And this do I judge is to be attributed unto nature herself, the best parent of all things: for since Egypt was destitute of dew and rain, nature in supply thereof gave thereunto this river which should be able to give nourishments unto corn and plants. For the divine providence of God hath appointed innumerable courses of rivers for the utility of the land and soil, through which their course lieth: because no country should be altogether without the help and furtherance of nature. For the increase of the river Nilus doth greatly benefit and help that country, because through the great overflowing thereof many hurtful beasts breeding there are thereby dispatched and drowned, except they speedily fly for refuge unto the higher places: unto which country alone these profits and commodities are incident, that it neither hath any clouds, nor cold winds, or any thick exhalations: the water thereof is very sweet, insomuch that the inhabitants there can easily live without wine, and can drink the same water with great pleasure.

I suppose the vicinity or nearness of the sea maketh much better for the preservation and safekeeping of a city, both for the use of civil life and also for the gathering together of riches, wherewith cities are marvelously increased: but those cities are far more harder to be besieged which the sea washeth upon, seeing that to the siege and expugnation thereof is required not only a great power by sea, but also a great army by land. Whereof if the one be wanting, the citizens may easily overcome the other host, when as it shall be hard for the army by land to send any succor unto the navy by sea: on the other part, the multitude or company of sea soldiers may easily be profligated and vanquished by horsemen. Therefore convenient and opportune havens must be carefully and wisely chosen out, by all them that would found and stablish a city.

Small fields and little arable grounds easily bringeth dearth of corn, which surely is the cause that thither is small recourse of people: for people pinched with penury and famine be afraid to marry, neither desireth to have any children, wherefore in suc ha country they do nothing increase: yea, rather the poorer sort, having respect to their neediness and famine, do forsake their country and seek to plant themselves in some pleasant and fruitfuller soil elsewhere, especially if their own country be so strait and narrow that it be not able to feed cattle: for next unto corn, cattle which greatly increaseth flesh, milk, and cheese, do best nourish. As for fishing, methinks it not greatly to be wished for, partly because that fishes do give ill nourishment to the body, and again do make men's bodies weak and sickly, which thing I may prove by Homer's testimony, who never made his warriors and soldiers, which encamped by the seashore, to taste or feed upon fish at any time: and again, because I do always see the fisherman to be chilling cold, bare, and needy.

Book 8

OF BUILDINGS, WALLS, GATES, CASTLES, FORTRESSES, GARRISONS, LIBRARIES, CHURCHES, AND OTHER MONUMENTS OF A CITY.

A NGELS, WHICH from the very nativity and birth, are appointed unto all men, are called the messengers of truth, which do sometimes foreshow and tell unto holy and innocent men, either sleeping or waking, such predictions and haps of things to come, as by event afterwards are found true.

A place that standeth high, or which hath ready windings and turnings, or which standeth either upon the sea or some great river, needeth far less labor and cost: for whereas the place is well defended by the natural situation of itself, it needeth the less walls: but plain countries or places not high must be succored and helped with labor and charges otherwise for defense. Regard also must be had of the height and thickness of the walls: for when the walls be very high, they are easily shaken and battered down with engines and guns: again where they are too low, they are easily conquered and scaled by the enemy with ropes and scaling ladders. Forty or fifty cubits high is of man cunning architects and skillful fortifiers allowed: in the top whereof that thickness is said to be sufficient, which may serve for two armed soldiers to go side by side, without hindering one another in meeting.

Moreover also there must be had very diligent consideration of the gates of a city, for by means thereof it chanceth sometimes, that by sudden uproars the towns be taken and sacked, or when the townsmen and citizens return or fly, the enemies being mingled among them may surprise the gates.

As Romulus at one incursion invaded and took the city of the Fidenatians, for he was purposed after that he had spoiled their fields to harry the country, drive away his prey, and so to have discamped with his host: but when the Fidenatians issued out of their city, there was between them a skirmish, wherein they being weaker were discomfited and put to flight. And thereupon Romulus, pursuing and chasing them, rushed into the city together with them that fled, as if they had been all of one company: and so was the city which he planted with Romans and brought under his own subjection. Regard therefore must be had that the ways of the gates be not direct or straight and forthright, but turning and winding many ways to deceive the enemies.

There hath been no small disputation amongst them which have writ of civil society, whether any tower or castle be fitly placed in a free city, in which thing this is to be considered, whether it do more good or evil amongst free citizens to have a strong fort committed to the credit and keeping of a few: and if we will truly judge of and throughly resolve the monuments of old histories, we shall find that most common weales and estates have been subverted and overthrown by negligence and treachery of them that have been the rulers and captains thereof, [rather] than have been preserved: and yet notwithstanding, Rome was taken and fired by the Frenchmen, but by the defense of the capitol was in part saved and at length with gold bought peace. But Aristotle affirmeth that a castle is unto a good common weale unprofitable and dangerous: and that it giveth opportunity unto tyranny, who doubteth Tymotheus that notable orator of Corinth plainly affirmed, that city which is kept by the garrison of a castle cannot lightly be without tyranny.

Pyrrhus king of Epyrotes on a time came to Athens and was with courteous hospitality of the citizens received: he after view taken of that city, abounding with exceeding great riches, and which was the mother of all laudable arts and disciplines, was brought into the castle of Pallas, and there did his solemnities with devoted reverence, beholding with great admiration the castle, how strong and impregnable it was both by natural situation and also by artificial fortification: at length when he was ready to depart and was now come into the marketplace, he rendered great thanks unto the rulers of the city which accompanied him, for the confidence and fidelity which they reposed in him: and finally warned them that they should never thenceforth give liberty and leave to any king to enter into their castle, lest after such entrance and view some peradventure using that good opportunity and hold should take the vantage, and thereupon invade their city. This counsel was very well liked of the Athenians as they which well knew how dangerous a thing it was for citizens to suffer stout and valiant men to enter into their chief fortress: and so from thence forwards they kept the gates thereof more diligently.

Private houses are to be built if it may be along the high streets on a row and or like proportion and making: for so they beautify and adorn the city. Neither let them build anything too much outward thereby to hinder any highways: for we must so live that a private house must be described to serve the use and commodity of the whole family. Neither let any vacant or unprofitable place be therein, and so the very view and sight thereof shall bring the more ornament thereunto: for as Cicero saith: the gorgeousness of a man's house augmenteth the dignity of the person dwelling in the same.

And I judge the covetousness of them to be worthy of great reprehension, who flowing and abounding in great wealth and riches, never bestow any cost in building, because they would spare their money and fill their chests for their posterity: whereas if our ancestors had followed any such order, we should until this day in our cities have had shepherd cabins and rustical cottages.

A library ought to be erected in some wholesome and quiet place, neither ought we to suffer our citizens to be defrauded and disappointed of such benefit: for if places of exercise which make for the health of men's bodies be in many cities with such carefulness and cost erected and appointed, how much more ought a library to be furnished and set forth which is the food of a well-nurtured mind and the exercise of a free or well-inclined nature. And if they that got the masteries or prizes in games deserved great honors—insomuch that standing in the company they were crowned with with the garland and crown of victory, and at their return into their own country were like triumphant victors, carried in chairs or wagons, and were also deemed worthy to be maintained with meat, drink, and apparel at the public charges of the cities perpetually—how much more are excellent learned men to be had in estimation, which do further and help the common weale as well in discipline and manners as also in their writings, by committing all things unto memory, which in time to come may profit their posterity.

Let such a place be chosen for a library whose prospect may be eastward, for the eyesight requireth morning light: for if it should either have prospect southward or westward, the winds blowing from thence would with their moist heat and warmness corrupt volumes and engender moths, which consume and eat books. Let the walls within the same be handsomely polished and trimmed, and let them be set out and beautified with green color, for all green things are good for the eyes and make the sight thereof sharp and quick.

Ptolomeus king of Egypt is highly commended, who finished and furnished a library at Alexandria to his inestimable charges and industry, in which library there were forty thousand volumes: all which books were destroyed by casualty of fire in the battle that Caesar had against Achiles lieutenant of the king's wars: for when as the king's navy, being by chance withdrawn, was commanded to be fired and burned: the flame thereof catched into a part of the city, and ragingly burnt all the houses wherein the books were laid. In which fire good learning and disciplines doubtless had a miserable and lamentable wreck. For the writers of all nations and countries did earnestly endeavor and strive to convey their books thither, as it had been into a theatre and mansion of wisdom and learning: of which library, if so much as the steps were extant, they should surely ease us of great labors and travails, and with the light of antiquity would clarify and lighten the obscure darkness of letters and disciplines.

We must also with great regard foresee that sacred houses or churches be edified and builded in fit and opportune places of the city, wherein we must first and chiefly consider this, that of churches and temples some be made for the most commodity of the citizens, some for the use of them that forsaking the world give themselves only to contemplation, which houses would be in some out corner or solitary place where they may not be interrupted and troubled with the busy tattling and civil tumult of the multitude, and therefore must be set out of the company and resort of men and out of the sight of private houses: and either be built in the territories, or else without the walls of the city. But those that are ordained for the public utility of the citizens ought to be situated in a fair room and place, either in the heart of the city or in the places that be best inhabited and peopled, to the intent the citizens may conveniently thither repair daily with their wives and children: but those churches which they call cathedral churches, whereof the bishop of the sea hath the rule and authority, all architects think most expedient to be builded upon an high ground in the midst of the city, that out of it the greatest part of the walls of the city may be viewed everywhere round about: for within the guard and protection thereof, the whole city seemeth to consist, and thither upon holydays all men flock together, as it were, unto a spectacle of divine and special matters. As for places in the churches and houses of prayer or preaching, where divine mysteries are to be celebrated, let them be ordained so far as may be best for the minsters and congregation: and if it may conveniently, eastward: but if the nature of the place will not so suffer it, let it be so and in such sort that it may stand in the full fight of the greater part of the church, wherein if they take advice of the skillful architects to oversee the workmanship, they shall build all things commodiously and orderly: neither shall they greatly stand in need of any my writing or precepts thereto, since the device and reason of building requireth rather a lively instructor than a dead director: moreover, that is true which as a common proverb is wont to be spoken, that an unskillful master or owner can a great deal better build in his own court or upon his own ground than a most learned and skillful workmaster in another. For man's diligence and long consideration of the owner or master surpasseth the device and skill of the artificer.

Book 9:

OF WARS AND MARTIAL DISCIPLINE. OF MUNITIONS, ORDINANCE, ARTILLERY, VICTUALS, MUSTERS, LIEUTENANTS, GENERALS, CAPTAINS, AND SOLDIERS. OF PEACE AND WAR, WITH THE CIRCUMSTANCES THEREOF.

T HERE IS nothing unto man's nature better than to be willing, neither anything greater, than to be able to benefit and help many. But forasmuch as the several wealth of many persons particularly is but slender and small, that although they would never so gladly, yet can they not extend liberality and requital towards them that well deserve: only kings and princes may be liberal, bountiful, and nobly minded.

Chilo the Lacedemonian, who was one of the seven wise sages of Greece, was abundantly enriched in a manner with all kinds of virtues, yet in nothing more than in beneficence and liberality: and therefore, when as he was come to extreme old age, oftentimes (as it were rejoicingly) he was wont to say, that in his lifetime he did never anything ingratefully: no virtue doth more commend and adorn captains, generals, and governors of armies than liberality, whereby they keep their soldiers constant and obedient in performing their duties, and also thereby allure and win their very enemies unto them, through hope of benignity and frankness.

The first onset and clasping together of the armies in fight is always counted dangerous and difficult: for true is that sentence of Scipio: that there appeareth greater courage and haughtiness in him that inferreth peril and adventureth to give the onset, than is in him that redefendeth: but after that open war be denounced, and that every man prepareth homeward out of his fields to stick to his safety and to stand circumspectly upon his garden, then they come together in their warlike order, and then they appoint their scouts, and marshal their soldiers, every man taketh stomach and courage unto him: he beholdeth and seeth his enemy, neither thinketh he it good and convenient to bicker disorderly and skirmishingly, but orderly and in good array: and then those matters which fear imagined to be dangerous, reason doth teach to be far less, and not so much to be doubted: then every man determineth with himself what is needful to be done, neither be they taken unprovided, nor receive the foil at their enemy's hands, but are every day more and more emboldened and encouraged, and by these means they commonly carry away the victory, which were provoked with injury afore: and thus do they many times revenge themselves upon their enemies and deliver their country from all thralldom and bondage.

But the order of waging battle is far more strait, and needeth deeper counsel: neither is it enough for us to consider that we go to fight in a righteous quarrel and for justly demanding our own right: and that for good causes war may well be waged and proclaimed: but we must also consider what our power is, and of what power and strength our adversaries and enemies are, what manner of soldiers we have, what partakers and confederates, what tributaries we have, and how they be affected towards us: to what sum our common stock or treasury amounteth to: for it is a thing odious and hateful to levy tribute upon private persons, and isa thing that very soon breedeth and getteth the envy of citizens. We must also consider how strong, how well fortified, and how well victualed the city is, with what garrisons the towns and castles within our jurisdiction be maintained and kept, and what store of munition and ordinance we have in our armory: these and many such like are before had to be prepared and weighed, and which are them chiefly acknowledged and best known when, the gates of the city being shut, the enemy is kept out and driven back from the walls with slings, arrows, and gunshot.

Advice, valiantness, and knowledge in martial matters be of great force and do much good in wars: but fortune chiefly excelleth all the rest, wherefore that sentence of Hannibal unto Scipio is true, where he saith: that the events of things never less agree and fall out according to our purposes than in war: and therefore an assured peace is better and safer than a victory which we do but hope for: also we must yield somewhat unto the multitude and vulgar sort, whose creedance always hangeth upon fortune and many times follow the minds of men mingled and gathered together out of sundry countries, whom no zealous piety or affection towards their country, no for of God nor religion keepeth in awe, but are only there allured with hire and stipendary wages.

All consultation of wars to be made upon others, although it be good for many purposes, yet in a free city is dangerous: for when the matter is referred to the senate, they do not all agree in one opinion; some follow the truth, and some frame themselves according to the opinion of the common people and be people-pleasers, advancing and setting forward the side which the vulgar sort best alloweth, and therefore the most part are deceived: for there is nothing amongst mortal men so unstable and wavering as the minds, wills, and opinions of the citizens, which not only being disallowed of (as Cicero saith) are angry and grieved, but also oftentimes do repine and grudge at things that be well done and by right and equity: therefore a wise man will advisedly deliberate and consider each circumstance before he absolutely give his consent to the enterprising of making wars, lest that he lay such a burden upon his shoulders under which he may fall down.

Labienus, a man fortunate and rich, who of his own proper costs and charges builded out of the ground the town called Cingulum in Picenum, took part too earnestly with Pompeius, wherefore he could not hope for any favor or pardon at the victor's hands, although indeed most merciful. For whether was an imparl and treaty of peace between the soldiers of Caesar and the soldiers of Pompei, this Labienus, with a loud voice, exclaimed and cried out saying: sirs, leave of to make any further talk of entreaty for peace, for except you first have Caesar's head from his shoulders, there can be no peace at all amongst you.

Nothing can be more dangerous in a free city than for a man to promise that he will be the author and ringleader of wars, which thing surely even they in mine opinion seem to do which openly in the counsel chamber aver that wars are expedient to be taken in hand. Solon was accounted a very wise man, yet he (because he would not freely give sentence that it was requisite to make wars against the Megarians for the recovery of Salamine) suddenly feigned himself mad, and, being disguised in apparel like a fool, provoked the Athenians to fight. When the matter fell out well, and that they had won Salamine, they all condemned and well allowed of his counsel and devise in that behalf: now Solon all this while, under shield of feigned madness shrouded himself, that if the matter should not have come to pass as he before had told them and as he would have it, yet thereby he might purchase pardon for his words and deeds.

It is oftentimes called in question, whether it be good to make wars for the increase and propagation of dominion and lordship, when any occasion of conquest is offered: or else whether it be better to be quiet and to live in peace: many arguments may be brought and alleged on both parts. But we rather incline unto peace.

Glorious truly is martial dealings, and I cannot tell whether there be anything more noble: and no man can deny but all great dominions and noble empires have been purchased and gotten by the attempt of wars. Without all doubt the renown and names of all most noble and flourishing cities should, for the most part, be buried in darkness, were they not made famous by martial feats. Neither hath the city of Athens attained so great fame or renown, which hath merited to have the name of the mother of all arts and disciplines, as Rome hath done: which was in times past the imperial seat of the whole universal world, although neither of the twain would seem to lack the others praise and commendation. For Rome itself excelled in the studies of all good arts and sciences, and Athens lacked the glory of warfare: for either of these cities bear great reverence unto the studies both of war and peace, and honored Minerva both armed and unarmed: but we (as I said before) do rather commend peace, and do especially desire to instruct our citizens in the same, because it leadeth more safely and surely unto the tranquility of mind. And therefore, living content with the territories and countries which we already enjoy, let us not enter into any wars but only such as is necessary, of if at any time we do enter into the same, let us as speedily as we can seek some way to bridle and qualify our desires: which thing even armed Hannibal seemeth to ratify, when as he said unto Scipio in this manner: it had been very good if the gods had given that mind unto our predecessors that you might be contented with the empires of Italy and we of Africa.

Vainglory and vain desire of sovereignty many times so inflameth men that they be contented with no territories or bounds, neither take they any felicity in peace.

Curtius writeth that the ambassadors of Scythia spake these words unto king Alexander: if the gods had given unto thee a body agreeable to the great greediness and ambition of thy mind, the whole world itself would not suffice to contain thee, thou wouldst with the one had touched the east, and with the other, the west, and having obtained all this, thou wouldst yet moreover know where and in what place the renown of such a stately majesty should be enthroned, and thus desirest thou the thing which thou canst not comprehend. From Europa thou travailest into Asia, and out of Asia again into Europa, finally if thou get the upper hand and overcome all human creatures and men living, then wilt thou makes wars with woods, clouds, rivers, wild beasts, and dumb creatures: what thinkest thou? doest thou not know that great trees do grow long time, and yet in one hour space they are plucked up by the roots? He is a fool that looketh after the fruits of them and measureth not the height of the tree, whereof they grow: take heed lest whilst thou strivest to come to the top of the tree, thou fall to the ground with the same boughs which thou layest hold upon.

Oh miserable state and condition of man. Oh deceiveable expectation which mortal natures have in this world. Why are we seduced and carried away with such greedy ambition, since we evidently see that all our goods and whatsoever worldly benefits else which we possess and enjoy are mutable, transitory, and frail, and that nothing is to be desired saving only virtue.

What do the subversions of cities gotten by conquest or otherwise avail? What do whole empires themselves profit us? but that only when we enjoy them, we do always live carking and careful? For true is that sentence of Julianus Caesar, who at the beginning of his reign, being troubled with tumultuous ruffling in France, said: that he had gotten nothing by being Emperor but only that he lived thereby, ever busy and occupied.

If we take in hand any wars, we must first forethink whom we may authorize and make the chief General and Captain: for if we will judge aright in this behalf, truly there can be nothing found more rare or difficult than a good General and Captain.

Philip king of Macedon said that he marveled why the Athenians did every year choose new Generals and Captains of their wars, since he in all his lifetime had found but one good Captain, namely Parmenio.

Cicero supposeth that four things ought to be in a chieftain or governor of wars: that is to say, knowledge or skill in martial matters: valiance: authority: and felicity: and unto these he addeth further: virtues (saith he) appertaining unto a General or chief Captain are travail and labor, fortitude and courage in dangers, industry in his dealings, quick dispatch in bringing things to pass, and advisement in forecasting with providence, which way to work his matters.

All men know that fortune lieth not in our power but is to be craved by prayer at the hands of God: but virtue and wisdom ought we to have at ourselves.

Cambyses (as Xenophon reporteth) advertised his son Cyrus that Captains of wars over and above all other soldiers should inure themselves to abide heat and drought, and in winter the storms and cold: and to be always at one end in all labors and dangerous adventures: forasmuch as the travels are not so grievous unto the Captain as the common soldier: for he that is a Chieftain or General ought to measure and by due consideration to weigh in his mind that fame and commendation in doing of exploits doth very much appertain unto him.

And it is expedience for him that hath the government of an armed host to inure young men to exercise, sometimes to go about watches: to see his soldiers victualed: to see the corn tried: to punish fraud and deceit in the measure there of, to punish faults, to be always present at the beginning: to hear the complaints of his soldiers: and to see the sick and diseased to be looked and provided for. There are also other virtues almost innumerable appertaining to a General, mentioned by such persons as have written of warlike affairs.

Soldiers that transgress or make offenses are to be punished, and with fear of the laws to be restrained: as those which scatter and wander abroad at random from the camp and so come again to their tents, and such as give the slip and go their ways, ranging abroad a long while, and afterward are brought again. For as the soldier which first fleeth is to be executed and put to death for example of the rest, so likewise is he to be punished which shall do a thing in wars that his Captain shall prohibit, or which observeth not the charge enjoined him, yea, although he otherwise worthily behave anc acquit himself: in which respect Manlius Torquatus in all ages is commended, who commanded his own son to be beheaded, because he presumed to fight against his commandment, and yet he fought stoutly and valiantly in defense of the common weale.

Generals and Captains shall do much more good with good example of their life and conversation than with the censure of manners or with any kind of cruelty. For Xenophon bringeth in Cyrus discoursing by way of oration, in manner to this effect: the chief work or part of a Prince or Governor is to show himself a man of honest conversation, and moreover to look that such as he has under his charge and at his commandment may prove virtuous and good men: and it is the duty of a soldier to obey his Captain willingly, to take in hand all labors, all adventures and dangers, not to fight but in array and according to prescription, to love his weapon, to have skill in warfare, and to set more by his honor, dignity, and good fame than by anything under the sun.

The laws of the Lacedemonians were very severe and sharp in martial matters, wherein (as Marcellinus declareth) those soldiers were sharply punished, which when the army was ranked and set in array, durst be seen to shroud themselves elsewhere under any roof or shed.

Writers report that Scipio, walking about with his friends, used to eat only cheat bread without anything else: and so do historiographers write that Masinissa king of Numidia used to dine, who being LXXXX years of age, used to dine standing or walking before his tent or pavilion. Such crimes specially have their original from the chief Governors and them that be in authority: for the soldiers do imitate the fashions and natures of those that have chief rule and governance over them: for if the Captains be good, they train their soldiers to goodness, but if they be ill, they then make their soldiers apt and prone to ill: for the multitude of the common soldiers are soon infected.

Soldiers are to be taught (by the example of Macus Cato) to be fierce and courageous against their enemies, and to show themselves gentle towards their friends and confederates, fearful to do injuries, but ready and prompt to revenge wrongs to them offered, and to desire nothing more than praise and glory, which indeed is a very goodly persuasion: for those that be desirous of praise do not shun nor refuse any travails, neither shrink they or withdraw themselves from any perils or dangers, but being inflamed with desire of glory, do nothing doubt to hazard themselves in all great adventures and dangers. Soldiers also must be punished that have done amiss: for too much lenity and favor doth make them more proclive and prone to dispense with all, but must punish those that are in the greatest fault: for if many be punished, they are to be sent and distributed to receive their execution in diverse places.

Marcellus upon a time openly perceived and saw Lucius Bantius Nolanus, a man very bold and factious, soliciting and stirring the townsmen there to revolt and turn unto Hannibal, and yet durst he not put him to death for fear of the Nolans: wherefore he called him unto him with fair words, praising him openly as a worthy soldier, and exhorting him to hold on and continue his good service and faithful loyalty, and to be willing still to bear out that warfare with him. And that the citizens should the better credit that he was in such favor with his Captain, Marcellus gave him a good fair courser, by means of which courtesy and gentleness he changed and altered the evil mind and treacherous disposition of Lucius, and thence forward found both him and all his retinue and crew trusty and faithful.

Many hold opinion that a General of an army ought not to combat and fight hand to hand with his enemy, except in time of great necessity, and that it is sufficient for him to perform the office of a Captain and leader, and not of a common soldier. For they say that cities have been utterly sacked and whole hosts slain down right, or at least discomfited and put to flight, by the rashness of their Captains and Generals: for while they pursue after every particular enemy, they forsake and leave the main host at all adventures, and while they study to take heed of one man's blow, they pull upon their own heads the whole main force of their enemies, not considering how that their own danger brings with it the general calamity and spoil of the whole host.

Scipio Africanus to certain men which said that he was no great fighter, wisely answered saying: My mother brought me forth into this world a Captain and a General, not a fighter or common soldier: thereby meaning that victory and conquest consisteth rather in the experience and wisdom of one than in the weapons and strength of many. Cyrus (as Xenophon mentioneth) asked Cambyses how a victory might best be gotten, to whom he thus answered: he that would win and have the upper hand and victory must entrap and take his enemies by all manner of policy whatsoever, either by secret ambushes or deceit and fraud, yea, by rapine, theft, and pilfery they must be spoiled, robbed, and impoverished: for nothing is to be pretermitted which may in any respect end to the subduing and vanquishing of a man's enemies: a very lie in convenient time by the chief Captain made hath suddenly obtained the victory: as that of Valerius Levinus, who with a loud voice cried out that he had slain Pirrhus, and therewithal to make the matter more credible held up his sowrd all bloody with the blood of a certain soldier whom a little before he had kileld, with which surmised lie the Epyrotes being suddenly astonied, ran away as fast as they could, weeping and trembling into their tents.

Demosthenes, the greatest orator among the Grecians, achieved many wars, and was in a great battle at Cheronea, wherein Philip of Macedon overcome the Athenians, out of which conflict Demosthenes by flight and running away saved himself: this thing being by way of reproach afterward laid in his dish, after the death of Philip, he excused himself by reciting this notable verse:

> *The party vanquished weeps and wails,*
> *But the party vanquishing by death quails.*

Julius Caesar, as he in worthy exploits surpassed all men, so also did he excel almost all the Romans in Latin eloquence. The knowledge also of histories is commodious and profitable for them which have the conduction and governance of armies, both because in taking counsels and advises, by the event and fortune of other men's former haps, most firm examples are learned, and again because the virtue that is praised in others doth allure and move us to obtain the like: and fearful cowardice, being reproved, doth make men become more valiant: and I cannot tell whether the knowledge of warfare may by any other discipline be better helped than by perusing historical monuments, by which we are taught and instructed to do all things well and orderly, which may either be spoken or thought by man. Nothing new and strange, nothing wonderful, nothing unheard or uncouth can happen unto the Chieftain, which hath very good knowledge and experience in histories.

Warlike order and array, discipline of soldiers, good respect and study in invading, and bewaring the enemy, skill in marshaling the army in right order of array, knowledge when to begin the skirmish, when to leave, how to plain ambushes and stales, and how to take heed of the like, which place is fit to be chosen, which place is most commodious to be first prevented and gained, which again is to be left unto the enemy, how and which way to give the onset and charge, and how to resist and stand at defense, with innumerable other points which scarce can be comprehended in long discourse, by what other means can they more easily be learned than by perusing over monuments and records of histories.

Among all sorts of men there can be nothing found more rare than a perfect Captain and General, which if he be not to be found in the city, he must be sent for from other places: for it is better to fight well and faithfully under a stranger Captain than in danger and hazard of life under the government of our native citizen.

He that hath the charge and authority over a city and in the time of war is also to look to urban affairs, and ought to employ very great diligence and to look narrowly unto his charge, that the city do not sustain any detriment or damage: and as (like a Captain in the camp) he ought to perform his office, so like a wise governor ought he to exercise and train his soldiers with the walls of the city that with idleness, niceness, sitting in the shade, and other delicate and tender cockerings of the city they be not effeminated. And sometimes it shall behoove himself in person to visit the wards and go through the watches, and not to commit all things to the disposition of them whom he maketh masters of the watches under him, who indeed shall keep their watch much more diligently and carefully, if they stand in fear and awe of him that is chief ruler over them all and see him to be watchful and vigilant. For there be which suppose that those persons are most sharply to be punished which negligently look to their watch and ward, lest by sleep, sloth, and negligence of one man the whole city should perish, which committeth all things to the diligence of those few persons: wherefore histories do highly commend Epaminondas the Thebane, who in time of great distress and danger, viewing and surveying in proper person the watches, thrust his sword through one of the watchmen, whom he found sleeping, saying these words: A deadman I found him, a deadman I leave him.

Neither is it to be marveled at, that Epaminondas, being otherwise a Captain gentle and merciful, did use and practice such severity upon a man sleeping, seeing that we do see how through such negligence whole cities have been sacked, spoiled, and burnt, whereupon Virgil saith:

Inuadunt urbe somno vinoque sepultam.

With wine and sleep, the city careless made,
The enemies do with force of arms invade.

By reason of this policy and diligence, Alcibiades above others is praised: for when the Athenians were by the Lacedemonians besieged, he gave warning unto the watchmen that they should well mark the light which he in the night season out of the tower or castle would show them, and that at the sight and beholding thereof they should also hold up another light: and if any were found remiss or negligent in doing accordingly, he should assuredly suffer punishment therefore, by means whereof he made the watchmen to become most diligent and wary.

Also there ought always to be scouts and especially to give warning in the night season by some beacon or flame of fire where the enemies approached, and in the daytime by smoke. Neither ought men to be suffered to go out at the gates into their fields till the scouts have throughly searched and tried, that they may safely go about their husbandry. Neither let the same scouts continue in their turns any long time, but daily let fresh men succeed in their rooms, lest with too much travail and tediousness they happen to handle their charge more negligently.

It is also very commodious and profitable that chief rulers and such as be in authority, either at home or in wars abroad, where some dangerous matters do chance, should go forth abroad in their own persons to see the state of things: by the example of Marcellus, who to his colleague or fellow in office, said these words: Let us ourselves go with a few horsemen to make search how the case standeth, for the thing manifested unto our eyes shall more certainly direct our advice and counsel what is best to be done. For Plato willeth Princes of common weals to go forth and see how things frame abroad, and with them to lead their children on horseback, thereby to inure them with less fear to abide the view and sight of their enemies.

The ancient custom that the Frenchmen used is very profitable, to learn and understand of all things which the enemy doeth and pretendeth: which custom many nations and Princes in our time also do use to put in practice, which is that some witty persons may be appointed to learn what fame and common report goeth abroad, and to make wayfaring persons (will they or nil they) to stay, and of them to learn and sift out what news everyone of them hath heard or known: let them inquire of them out of what coasts or countries they came, and whither they mean to go, and let them compel them to declare as much as they known of their pretense to come. But yet such news, flying tales, and reports they may not always credit: for many do tell lies and do feigningly answer according to the will and humor of him that asketh the question, and so leave the demanders as wise (for any certain) as they were before: but if the demanders and sifters out of these matters be circumspect and wise, they shall easily be able to bolt and try out the truth, and thereby their counsels and advises, which are to be daily taken in hand, shall by such examination be much the better furthered.

Let also the Lieutenant or Governor of a city and citizens be very diligent and circumspect in the safekeeping and guarding of the gates, the keys thereof let him keep himself, and let him set in good order the watches and wards duly: let him also take heed that he be not deceived and dissembled withal under the color of his own soldiers, or beguiled by the counterfeiting of an other known speech. For Hannibal surprised many cities in Italy by appareling and arming his soldiers like Romans, sending before him such of his soldiers as by long continuance in the wars could speak the Latin tongue. Many subtle shifts and deceits are devised in the entrance of the gates of a city, which are to be taken heed of. For sometime the enemies for the nonce and of set purpose do make their beasts and carriages to fall down, or else their waynes that carry great huge stones to break and fall in pieces, and thereupon the enemies being suddenly at hand (while the gates cannot well be shut) the towns are easily taken. The Massilians, fearing this thing, by the good instructions and ordinances of their common weale, did so keep and ward their cities in time of peace as if they had then been continually vexed and troubled with wars:

wherefore upon the holydays they were wont to shut the gates of their cities, to keep their watches, to see their soldiers in good array standing upon the walls to muster and take a not of their strangers and other warlike affairs beside.

Revolts and runagates are not to be received or entertained into the city: for Synon the Grecian, being gently entertained, was destruction of the Trojans. And Zopirus the friend of Darius king of Persia, perceiving the king to wax weary with his long besieging of Babylon, and being without all hope of winning it, cut off his own nose and his own ears, and fled away thence unto the Babylonians, where he uttering many slanderous and reproachful words against his king, promised them that he would deliver into their hands the victory and be avenged on him. They, believing his smooth words, made this Zopirus their General Captain and delivered unto him their power, which when he had received, incontinently he betrayed and delivered both the city and the whole host unto Darius. So also Sextus Tarquinius, feigning himself to have fled away from his father's host, because he was (as he had feigned) beaten with rods, and, coming to the city of Gabij (then besieged), persuaded them to join in like hatred with him against the king his father, and being by them appointed chief Captain, he straightways betrayed the city into the hands of his said father.

It is also dangerous to retain many strangers and alien into the city: both because every multitude of people that is gathered and pieced together out of sundry nations is unquiet and oftentimes of a small matter or quarrel stirreth up tumults and hurlyburlies: but also because it is the part of a madman to divide there those things amongst many which he knoweth not whether they will suffice to the maintenance of a few.

Unto this sentence may be aptly applied that same precept of Cambyses king of Persians, which he gave unto Cyrus his son, where he saith:

No man ought to stay till poverty oppress,
But rather to provide in time of wealthiness.

Alexander of Macedon, besieging Leucadia, suffered all the borderers and neighbors thereabout to fly thither for refuge and succor, that they being many might the sooner consume the victuals, which being spent, he easily obtained the victory. Antigonus seemeth to have used the like device against the Athenians, who having destroyed their corn fields, departed thence, and went away in the time of seed sowing, that if they had any remainder of corn left they might bestow the same upon sowing: and so making his return thither again the next spring, overcame and spoiled all the corn being now sprouted and shot up: and so by famine brought them to agree to anything, even at his own pleasure.

The multitude also of soldiers is greatly to be feared, this the Cathaginians apparently taught: for when they had made peace with the Romans, the mercenary soldiers, which were in number about 20,000 and fought against the Romans, conspired together and revolted and fled from the Carthaginians, and beside this, inveigled and seduced all Africa: and thereupon besieged Carthage and could not be kept from scaling the walls, had not the labor and industry of Hamilcar, then the chief Captain of Carthage, been the greater.

Let a Chieftain make dispatch and haste in those matters there he is bent and fully persuaded to doe: for speedy expedition is the best companion in warfare: in which thing, Alexander of Macedon is especially commended, because in expedition and speediness he surpassed the celerity and haste of all other Captains: and he had so framed his footmen that they were as swift and nimble on foot as horses: wherefore Darius the king being by him pursued, chased, and persecuted, grievously complained that he had no time of respite given him to pause and consider how to withstand the alacrity of Alexander, who oftentimes courageously traveled with great journeys night and day to entrap his enemies at unawares, and to set upon them suddenly and unlooked for.

Let also the chief Captain of the wars do his matters closely and secretly, and let him not open and disclose his secrets unto any man, by the example of Metellus, who, as Plutarch mentioneth, thus answered a certain friend of his which demanded of him what he would do the next day following: If this my coat which I wear (saith he) could utter forth and openly declare my secrets and determinations, I would straightways put it off and burn it to ashes. And Julius Caesar, purposing to transport and send his army another way, took his journey secretly, and delivered to some one man his tables, signed with his hand, directing them at a certain time and place to be ready, and in good array of battle to do what he should command them: and now and then commanded the notes to be written upon stones lying in the highways, where his soldiers must pass, whereby he gave them by certain watchwords directly to understand what way was needful and best to be taken.

As it is the part of a good physician to leave no hurtful thing in the body of his patient, so it is the part of a good General to remove and take away whatsoever shall hinder the prosperous estate and preservation of this his authority: for oftentimes it falleth out that a small spark of fire being neglected and not looked unto causeth a great flame, as the proverb saith. And that sentence of Marcus Cato is to be holden for an oracle, writing thus in his Book of Warfare: In other matters (saith he) whatsoever is misdown may be redressed or afterwards at more leisure amended, but in war, we must not admit the promise of any amendment for faults committed, because present punishment ought out of bad to follow the offense. For the revenger of sloth and ignorance is evermore at hand ready and pressed, which is never favoring or pitiful towards the enemy that offendeth.

There are two precepts which seem to contain in them the whole discipline or art of warfare: the one is that there be but few Governors or Commanders, and the same able well to govern, and them also such as have passed through all the degrees of warfare, whereby by obeying aforetime themselves they have the better skill to command others. They which have these things, it cannot be chosen, but that they shall either obtain the victory or else an honest and honorable peace: but to them which fail in these things, no power or force can suffice for their defense, but they shall be carried headlong with a blind rage to their utter ruin and destruction, even like brute beasts.

Clemency and mercifulness towards their subjects and underlings both greatly set forth the commendation of Generals and Captains, and maketh their noble acts more famous. Cicero affirmeth that they are to be received into favor and protection which with submission cast down their weapons and betake themselves to the mercy of the General, yea, although the ordinance and engine have shaken or battered down the wall.

And Caesar was wont to say that nothing pleased him better than to spare the simple sort of people, neither is this virtue to be omitted towards those which are overcome and vanquished: for slaughter, lust, cruelty, and every example of outrageous pride towards those that be in distress and misery, hath been always accounted detestable and horrible: great commendation did Marcus Marcellus win, who before he would grab the spoil of the wealthy city Syracuse, unto his soldiers wept, and by an edict commanded that no man should hurt or injure any freeman of the city. Livius maketh mention that the spoil of the city was so exceeding great, that there would have been scarcely the like in Carthage, which was of power and equal strength always to encounter with them.

In mine opinion, this note or precept is expedient to be given, that we should far more esteem of a small number of soldiers being trained up and exercised in the feats of war and sooner should gain the victory, than of a great multitude which are both unskillful and ignorant, who do upon and, as it were, make a ready way to their own destruction, who are afraid of every trifle, and rather take care for flight than for glory or renown: therefore the old precept willeth a man that lacketh an old beaten soldier to take a novice as yet untrained.

For Alexander after the death of his father Philip, with forty thousand tall armed soldiers that had been by his father notably and skillfully trained in feats of wars, overcame sundry and innumerable hosts of his enemies that withstood him, and subdued very many regions and countries of the world under his subjection, and compelled them to be come vassals unto him.

What shall we say of the Romans, who being descended from mean beginnings, yet by virtue and prowess only and by martial skill, did conquer all the whole world? Is it not a thing to be marveled at, that a number of herdmen and shepherds should invade Italy, a country most mighty above all other regions, and daunt and subdue the Germans and all France: despising the largeness of their bodies and the number of their hosts, and besides this should also tame and bring in subjection the Spaniards, which were right fierce and cruel warriors, and should conquer and vanquish the Africans, which were the wiliest and wealthiest persons under the sun: and moreover, should overreach the wisdom and cunning of the Greeks, and finally become Lords of the whole world?

In the choice and mustering of persons apt for the wars, we must first and foremost have a respect unto the age of the person, which ought to be young and tender. For boys and striplings do far more easily learn those things which are expedient, and do better frame themselves to things wherein is no difficulty, while their members are not yet stiff and hardened, neither grown to their full strength and perfection: for they sit a horse better and they handle the reins nimbler than aged persons with stooping bodies, whose limbs be stiff and hardened. And furthermore lightsomeness in leaping up and down, swiftness in running, and quickness in casting, is more easy for the body, which yet is tender and green, than for a body that is grown unto full strength.

Surely Plato, prince of all philosophers, held opinion that young men were to be chosen for the wars at the age of twenty years, and Servius Tullius king of the Romans, was of opinion to choose them at seventeen years old, at which age he called them *Iuuenes*, because they were persons able to help and aid their country and common weale. Some others do write that the first years of puberty, that is when the hairs do beginneth first to grow, is the best time to choose on that we would have to prove a worthy servitor. But the soldiers which are taken up being about the age of [xvii?] years, are seldom commodious. And when they handle their weapons, because they do it unhandsomely, they are but made laughing stocks unto others, and oftentimes because of their unwieldiness they are by the old [much?] quipped, which saith: that they be as fit for warfare as an ox to bear a pack saddle: therefore it were better to exempt such and remit them to such arts as they have been brought up in, than to press them to the wars where they will serve to small purpose, except it be in great necessity: for then we read that prisoners and malefactors have been loosed out of prison and set at liberty, and bondmen also in this case to have served for the present turn. Conelius Celsus writeth that a square bodied personage is most serviceable, and he praiseth a mediocrity of breadth and length: because tallness in youth is comely, is by nature soon consumed and brought to an end by old age. But as the stature which tendeth unto mediocrity is firmer, stronger, and of longer continuance, so on the other part, a slender body is counted weak and feeble, and a fat body is thought to be dull and unwieldy: notwithstanding I know that some do best allow of tallness in a soldier, whereupon the Romans [had?] their lively and courageous horsemen, and in their first bands [or raids] and cohorts suffered none to serve but those that were in stature six foot or very near thereunto.

Neither am I ignorant that Alexander and his host, by reason of their small stature, were at their coming into that country derided and laughed to scorn of the Scythians, which were very tall persons, but when a small time after, the Scythians learned that manliness and courage, and not tallness and height, was to be considered in the esteem. For it many times comes to pass that little persons and men of small stature prove and are found the best warriors.

Therefore, we must not stand upon this point, to consider how tall a man be, but how strong he is: yet notwithstanding the confirmation and well knitting of the members together may give great tokens of strength in man. Let therefore a young man that is to be employed this way be wall visaged and straight bodied, round necked and handing somewhat downward, quick eyed and watchful, cheerly countenanced, broad breasted and broad shouldered, strongly drawned in his arms and firmly compacted in the joints of his fingers, long armed, strong elbowed, slender bellied, big hipped, his legs rather slenderly than roundly calved and strongly fasted.

Moreover, in levying and mustering soldiers, we must consider in what country they were born and brought up. For albeit in every place there be born as well dastards as valiant and stout persons, yet notwithstanding the aspect of the heavens, furthereth much unto the courage and strength of the person: and the north countries are better in this respect than the easterly: but every temperate country is reputed and taken as best.

A soldier is better taken out of the country than out of the city, as all the ancient writers which have written of warfare do hold opinion: and not without good cause: for the country youth being hardened and sunburned, suffering and enduring dust, rain, and snow, feeding upon bread and wild bears, can abide far more easily to live abroad, can suffer rain, showers, and storms, can continue to roam through the stippery and dirty fields all barefooted which no horse can pass for mire and foulness, much better than tenderly brought up young men can, which have been cockered and nicely effeminated with town delicacies and pleasures of the city, which cannot sleep except they may lie upon a soft feather bed, where no noise must disquiet or trouble them, and being not able to endure either heat or cold, are ever pewling in their stomach, they never have good appetite to their meat except they may have the delicate dishes of the city fare and dressed after the city fashion, ever seeking for the finest broths and viands, neither can they be at heart's ease if they want their old domestical blandiments. Furthermore nature herself prescribeth this unto mankind, that he less feareth wounds or death which hath least knowledge of delicacies and pleasures in this life.

The Lacedemonians deserved great praise and commendation in warfare, whose life, if we do behold, we shall find that even till the age of [man's?] state were occupied and busied in the fields and in hunting and always lived very strictly and hardily.

The ancient Romans esteemed the care of warfare and husbandry as one: and the selfsame persons in time of peace played the husbandman, did in time of war serve for soldiers:

whereupon Quinctius Cincinnatus was called from the plough to be dictator, and after the victory gotten over his enemies, he surrendered his room and dignity, and returned to his oxen and small plot of land which he had at home. So likewise Fabricius, after he had expelled Pyrrhus out of the coasts of Italy, and Marcus Curius, surnamed Dentatus, having vanquished the Sabines, betook themselves again to their fields.

Also Curius Marcus long time after was a Captain chosen out of the country, and yet was he seven times consul and with many and great victories was his fame ennobled, and so hardened was he in labor and painstaking that when he offered his legs (being swelled) to the surgeon to be cut off and lanced, he did it with no more fear than he would have given a carpenter a piece of timber to be squared: this last of all is to be concluded, that the harder and painfuller that the trades be which men do commonly practice and follow, the stronger and stouter do the same make the soldiers: and the nicer and finer that they be, the more do they weaken courage and abate valiantness. For it is not to be looked for, that cur dogs which come peaking out of taverns and tippling houses should give the onset upon a leopard or lion, nay, they will rather straightway return to the licking of their dishes again.

The exercise of hunting is very good, which differeth much from rustical and warlike affairs: for Xenophon when he determined to follow the wars of Cyrus did first with great care and diligence learn to ride and hunt, affirming that he was an unprofitable soldier which was not in both these exercises greatly inured and practiced. For the Romans—because their young men should not give themselves too much to pleasure or be marred with idleness and ease in corners and bookiness—made a goodly field for exercise, which they called Campus Martius, wherein the games and exercises of arms were celebrated and kept, not only for the spectacles and sights of fencers and swordplayers, but also for the use and exercise of soldiers: and thereat were present certain that instructed and trained the same soldiers, which were with the common charge and provision recompensed with double shares of grain and corn: because they should the better and diligentlier (being inflamed with reward) train and teach the same soldiers.

It would ask a long discourse to make rehearsal of all martial exercises, and orderly to describe the rules and methods thereof, to set down precepts how young soldiers should be trained, how they should behave themselves in avoiding and declining weapons coming towards them, and how to deal prudently and manfully in striking again, how they ought to play the parts of soldiers throughly in every point: how they shall handle the shield or target: how to set and pitch their stakes, observe their array in marching, and keep their standings, all which things rather seem to appertain unto him that writeth of warfare than unto him which entreateth of civil society.

Plato setteth down in order that no man should have authority in the wars before he were thirty years of age, although there were otherwise in him approved and tried manhood and valiance, and that he were also even at those years ennobled or made famous for some martial exploits. This age did the Athenians think lawful and fitting for warlike offices, although sometimes they derogate from this law, especially in Alcibiades, who in his adolescence was so highly in the people's favor that wheresoever he walked abroad all the citizens cast their eyes only upon him, and no man so well esteemed amongst them all as he was. For before he was of lawful age, he was made Lieutenant General of the wars against the Syracusians, unto whom notwithstanding were adjoined two colleagues far elder than himself, that is to say Nicias and Lamachus, to the end they might more safely provide for the public weale. Also Octavius Caesar, at the age of XVIII years, was elected Emperor, Cicero persuading the same unto the people of

Rome, but afterwards when he handled some matters against the mind and liking of Cicero, he was sorry for that which before he had done and repented his former counsel and advice which he had given for his advancement and election, and thereupon wrote an epistle, wherein he exclaimeth against himself that he had played no wiseman's part, but confessed that the common weale was by him and through his means deceived.

Far more safe is an army or host committed unto old beaten soldiers than unto young men, whose first advisements and counsels are more fierce and unstayed, and who do less foresee and consider the uncertainty of chances, because fortune never at any time deceived them: but old men with quiet minds do foresee many things, and prevent beforehand how to encounter with fortune: and where need is of stout persons, they do the same, not so willingly as driven thereunto by necessity, and will rather choose to die in fight than in flight.

Alexander king of Macedon being twenty and one years of age lost his father Philip by death, and because he would seem to be no less the heir and successor of his kingdom than of his worthiness and glory, when as he had taken on him the government of the army left him by his father, he did not choose unto him those companions which he had been brought up and conversant with, neither youthful yonkers: but old tried and beaten soldiers: many of them such as were already discharged and dispensed withal from following the wars any longer, who aforetime served his father and had abided many a sharp storm under him: in which doing, he seemed rather to have chosen masters ans captains of wars than soldiers: and he committed not the ordering and disposing of his battles but unto them that were LX years of age, which surely was the cause that he always vanquished the enemy and obtained the victory, and with a very small band of men overcame six hundred thousand of the

Persians: and if he had not been by death prevented, he surely would have subdued the whole world.

The Tribune or Marshall of the field ought to be a man most valiant and courageous, in prowess and martial chivalry exactly trained: the rulers also of every particular crew or band, which have so many men at their commandment, ought in their office to be persons most grave, because that in the absence of the General they supply his room. He also that hath the charge and office of pitching the tents and encamping, ought of all others to be most skillful, and one by long experience and practice in wars throughly tried and experienced. For he ought diligently to view and survey the nature and condition of the place, that he may choose the safest and most convenient parts for the army to camp in that there be no hill or ridge where his soldiers might be easily by the enemy assaulted and displaced, neither by means of a river surrounded and drowned, or else by the too much nearness of wood growing thereabout to be consumed and fired, which thing happened unto Crassus in the civil wars, who through such careless oversight was with all his army almost burned suddenly by the fire that his enemies had secretly enkindled. So did Camillus also destroy and spoil the camp and tents of the Volscias by firing the wood that was near unto them.

Moreover let a General foresee that there be store enough of wood, of forage, of water: let them also have an easy egress abroad into the fields round about them, and a safe return and egress back again to the camp. Neither ought the surveyor or chief overseer of workmen to lack long experience, upon whom chiefly resteth all the charge, to see that nothing be wanting to the host that is needful, either for assault and battery, or for repulsing or defense. This man ought to have in a readiness carpenters, loigners, rafterers, and masons, for the contriving and making of engines and wooden towers, bettering pieces, crossbows, slings, and other sorts of guns besides: and briefly to conclude, the ancient persons must be appointed rulers over the army, and the younger sort must be honored with other dignities, and specially such as have more glory and praise when the case falleth out well and with good success, the danger [being] if it should fall out otherwise or that fortune should deceive them. Reward and punishment are to be deemed and taken as two gods in a common weale, and in martial affairs especially accounted most necessary: for neither shall it be sufficient for a Captain to keep his soldiers at commandment and in obedience for fear of punishment, except also the hope of glory and reward do quicken and prick forward the courage and fortitude of the soldier: and the desire of renown doth of itself particularly prescribe such things as neither the leaders nor Captains themselves can by any possible means direct or teach. For surely hope is a right great affect and motion of the mind, which oftentimes stirreth up and moveth men to do those things which seem to exceed the strength and ability of man, and which otherwise could not by any reason or means be persuaded.

FINIS.

Other books currently available from Sacra Press:

A Treatise of Christian Religion
by Thomas Cartwright
Father of the Puritans & of Presbyterianism displays the full jewels of a systematic theology in a catechetical format. Newly republished for the first time in centuries.

The Old Faith
by Henry Bullinger
Titanic Swiss Reformer weaves a mixed work of biblical & covenant theology, born of pastoral concerns, to prove the antiquity of the Christian Faith.

Lectures On Human Nature
by Samuel Doak
18th century American Presbyterian, church-planter, and school teacher keenly pens an introductory philosophy of human nature. Includes his sermon to the Overmountain Men just before their victory at King's Mountain.

A Precept for the Baptism of Infants
by Nathaniel Stephens
17th century non-conformist Minister proves the precept of paedobaptism from the New Testament in response to the objection of anti-paedobaptists.

The Cambridge & Saybrook Platforms
by Miscellaneous Ministers
New England Congregationalists inscribe their polity.

Books soon-to-be or now published by Sacra Press:

On the First Sin of Adam
by Franciscus Junius
French Protestant Reformer and theologian explores Adam's first sin and its relation to God's foreknowledge and decree, necessity, and free will.

The System of Political Discipline
by Bartholomew Keckermann
Late 16th century German Reformed scholar, philosopher, and theologian masterfully and methodically constructs an impressive, systematic work of political theory.

The Christian Obligations of Citizenship
by John G. Sheppard
19th century Anglican academic exploits logic, rhetoric, history, classical sources, and Scripture to construct his Christian political theory.

Positive Christianity in the Third Reich
by Cajus Fabricius
Protestant Theologian and NSDAP party member writes to show the compatibility between National Socialism and a certain form of Christianity. Includes The 28 Theses of the German Christians.

With many more to come—Lord willing.

Visit www.sacrapress.com/armory to purchase available books, to stay updated on releases, and more.